FIND STEPHEN'S
BROTHER ON PAGE 42

CHILDREN OF BRITAIN JUST LIKE

ME

PUT YOUR OWN PICTURE
OF YOURSELF HERE

THIS BOOK BELONGS TO ME
MY NAME IS

....

FIND SARA LEE
AND HER SISTERS
ON PAGE 20

CHILDREN
OF BRITAIN
JUST LIKE ME

BARNABAS AND ANABEL
KINDERSLEY

(with assistance from Maximilian)

DK

LONDON • NEW YORK • SYDNEY • DELHI

DORLING KINDERSLEY

www.dk.com

Created by Leapfrog Press Ltd

Editor Miriam Farbey
Art editors Miranda Kennedy,
Catherine Goldsmith

Production Lisa Moss
Picture research Liz Moore

Published in Great Britain by Dorling Kindersley Limited,
9 Henrietta Street, London WC2E 8PS

2 4 6 8 10 9 7 5 3 1

Copyright © 1999 Dorling Kindersley Limited, London
NMEC logo © NMEC 1998

Details of the royalties payable to UNICEF
can be obtained by writing to the publisher,
Dorling Kindersley Limited, at the above address.

A CIP catalogue record for this book is available from
the British Library.
ISBN 0-7513-7102-5

Colour reproduction by Colourscan, Singapore
Printed and bound in Italy by Graphicom

SARA LEE 20

STEPHEN 42

KERRY ANN 58

TJ 34

SAMANTHA 12

RHIANNON 44

RUAIRIDH 8

SAMANTHA 52

JOJO 46

INDERJIVAN 16

RUDI 54

PHILLIP 28

LISA 56

CAN 62

CEM 62

RUBY 38

CARL 22

MICHAEL 40

DOUGLAS 18

OLLIE 50

FRANCESCA 14

KIERAN 10

THOMAS 36

NICOLA 32

HELENE 24

ALICE 30

unicef

"The kids are our future - celebrate the Millennium Experience!"

The children of the millennium live in every corner of the world. As you can read in the wonderful pages of this book, they lead very different lives and come from all sorts of backgrounds but yet they share so many of the same hopes and dreams for the future.

Through the UN Convention on the Rights of the Child, UNICEF wants to give every child, wherever they may live, the right to a safe, healthy and happy childhood.

I've been lucky enough to see, at first hand, UNICEF's work in war-torn Sri Lanka and know how hard they are trying to give kids a better future in the new millennium.

Robbie Williams

UNICEF
Ambassador

LOOKING BACK

1946 UNICEF, the United Nations Children's Fund, was set up to help children in the aftermath of World War II. Its work expanded from the 1950s to help children in developing countries. We enter the new millennium as global citizens. The needs and rights of children, whether they are from Britain like those in this book or elsewhere in the world, have never been more important.

Robbie Williams is a UNICEF supporter who raises funds for Music for UNICEF. He says, "Join us and help UNICEF turn battlegrounds into playgrounds."

1949 The first UNICEF charity card was painted on glass by a Czechoslovakian girl, as a thank you for the help UNICEF had given her village during World War II. Since 1949, UNICEF has sold over 3.5 billion charity cards.

1981 UNICEF launched a big immunization campaign in 1981. At that time, under 20% of the children of the world were immunized against diseases which could kill them. Since 1990, 80% of children are now immunized against diseases like measles, TB, tetanus, diphtheria, whooping cough and polio. Polio has now nearly been eradicated from the world – once it is, it will join smallpox as being a disease of the past.

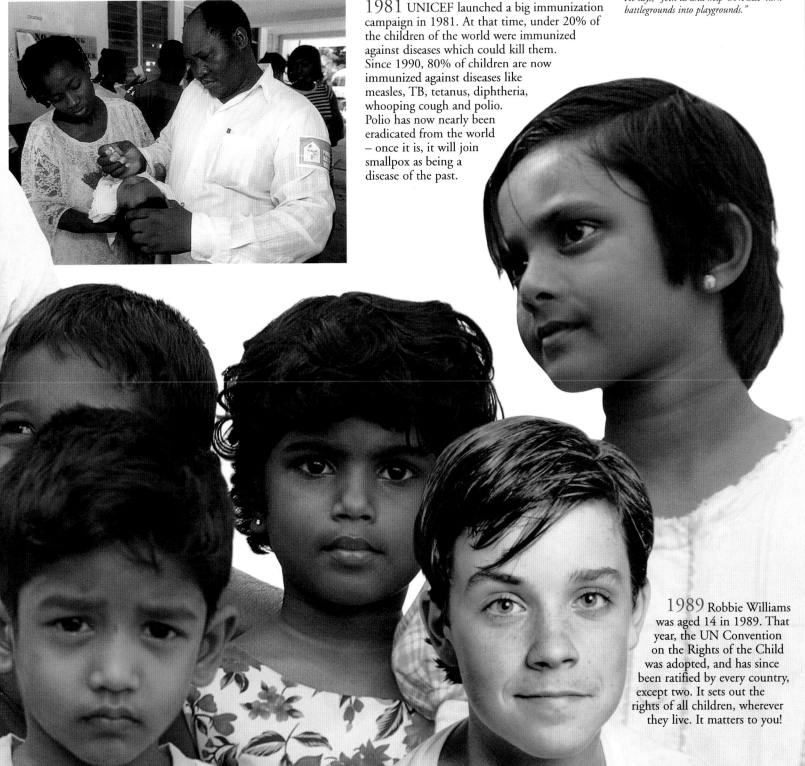

1989 Robbie Williams was aged 14 in 1989. That year, the UN Convention on the Rights of the Child was adopted, and has since been ratified by every country, except two. It sets out the rights of all children, wherever they live. It matters to you!

Ruairidh

"We don't have a TV – we don't need one. We've got lots of things to do."

Eight-year-old Ruairidh (pronounced roo-a-ri) lives in Applecross, a remote peninsula in northwest Scotland. Ruairidh's father, Alasdair, is a fisherman, as Ruairidh's grandfather and great-grandfather were before him. Ruairidh leaves Applecross to visit his grandfather in the nearby Kyle of Lochalsh, or every couple of months, to go shopping in Inverness, two hours' drive away.

THE HIGH ROAD
The main road into Applecross is called the Bealach Na Ba, which means "the pass of the cattle" in Gaelic. It is one of the highest roads in Britain, at some points as high as 625 metres. Until recently, the Bealach was the only road into Applecross. In 1976, a new road was built connecting many houses around the coast.

FISHERMAN
Alasdair goes out in his boat at 7 a.m. to haul creels, or nets, full of prawns from the seabed. He also farms scallops. He catches eggs in nets in the sea, then transfers them to wire and net "lanterns" hung from ropes into a lake. At two years old, he transfers them to the seabed. At five years old, he dives for them.

Fishermen wear orange or yellow waterproof suits so that they will be seen if they fall overboard.

Alasdair hauls 700 of his 1,400 creels a day and catches 60–120 kg of prawns. Most of his catch is exported live to Valencia in southern Spain.

Creel

Prawns swim in through the holes to eat bait. They can't work out how to get out.

UPPER TOSCAIG
Ruairidh's house is in Upper Toscaig on the edge of Applecross. The house has been in his family for generations. He and his brothers swim in the burn (the Scots word for stream) nearby. Their favourite game is to plug holes in a polystyrene fish box with modelling clay, then float down the burn on the box.

This is an elderly lobster that Alasdair caught by mistake. He felt sorry for it and threw it back in the sea.

Ruairidh, age 8

Kenny, age 10

Ruairidh and his brothers like to bury each other in the huge sand dune at Sand Hill.

Niall, age 4

Calum, age 11

Ruairidh's mother, Alison

CATCHING CRABS
Alasdair and the boys like to search for crabs under stones. They catch them for fun, then let them scurry away.

SPEAKING GAELIC
Ruairidh's grandparents speak the native Scots language, Gaelic. Ruairidh uses some Gaelic words, such as *seanair* (pronounced shennar: grandfather), *tapadh leat* (tapa-let: thank you) and *ciamar a tha thu* (kimmera-a-ha-oo: how are you). Ruairidh means "red" in Gaelic.

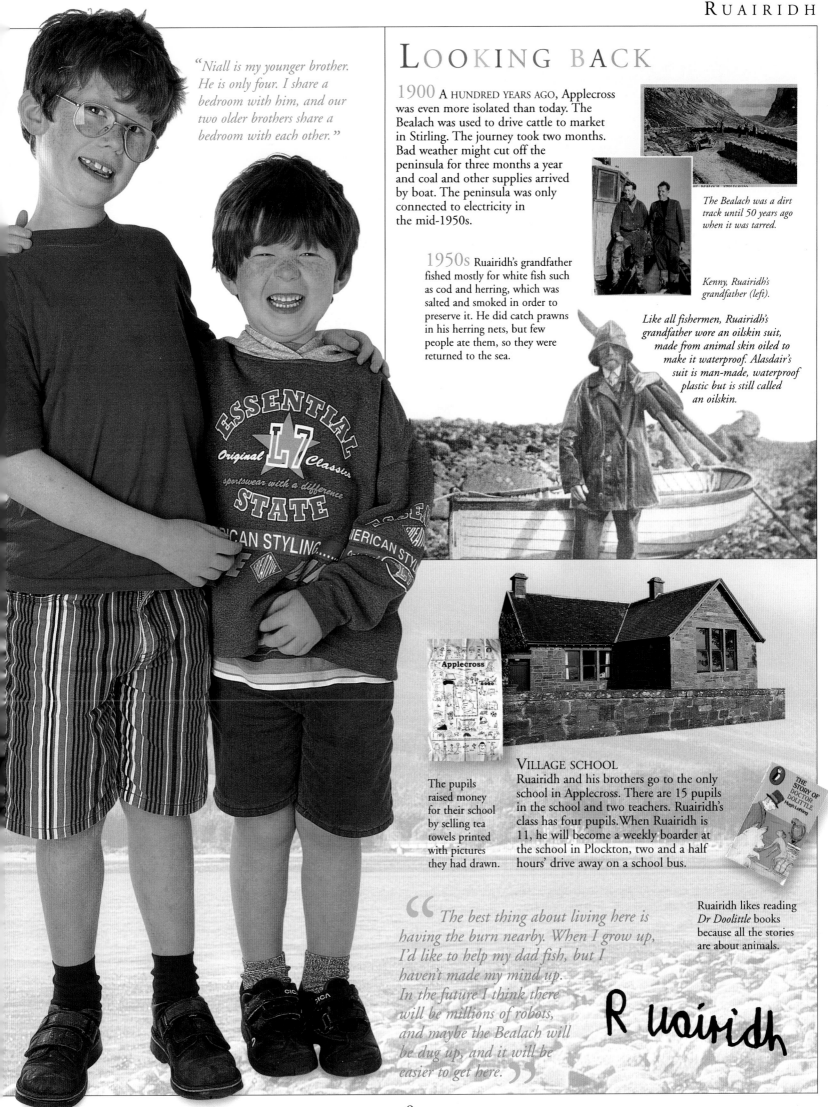

"Niall is my younger brother. He is only four. I share a bedroom with him, and our two older brothers share a bedroom with each other."

LOOKING BACK

1900 A HUNDRED YEARS AGO, Applecross was even more isolated than today. The Bealach was used to drive cattle to market in Stirling. The journey took two months. Bad weather might cut off the peninsula for three months a year and coal and other supplies arrived by boat. The peninsula was only connected to electricity in the mid-1950s.

The Bealach was a dirt track until 50 years ago when it was tarred.

1950s Ruairidh's grandfather fished mostly for white fish such as cod and herring, which was salted and smoked in order to preserve it. He did catch prawns in his herring nets, but few people ate them, so they were returned to the sea.

Kenny, Ruairidh's grandfather (left).

Like all fishermen, Ruairidh's grandfather wore an oilskin suit, made from animal skin oiled to make it waterproof. Alasdair's suit is man-made, waterproof plastic but is still called an oilskin.

VILLAGE SCHOOL

The pupils raised money for their school by selling tea towels printed with pictures they had drawn.

Ruairidh and his brothers go to the only school in Applecross. There are 15 pupils in the school and two teachers. Ruairidh's class has four pupils. When Ruairidh is 11, he will become a weekly boarder at the school in Plockton, two and a half hours' drive away on a school bus.

" The best thing about living here is having the burn nearby. When I grow up, I'd like to help my dad fish, but I haven't made my mind up. In the future I think there will be millions of robots, and maybe the Bealach will be dug up, and it will be easier to get here. "

Ruairidh likes reading *Dr Doolittle* books because all the stories are about animals.

Ruairidh

Kieran

Ten-year-old Kieran lives on Guernsey, one of the Channel Islands situated between Britain and France. Kieran's father, Nigel, is a market gardener who grows tomatoes, a typical occupation in Guernsey. Kieran has plenty of space to play around his father's large greenhouses. To earn pocket money, Kieran and his two sisters help pick the tomatoes, which are packed in crates and sold to supermarkets.

"I like the space here. I can play football on my own pitch and ride my ponies."

VAZON BAY
Kieran lives 10 minutes' walk from Vazon Bay, one of Guernsey's many beautiful and unspoilt beaches. His grandparents live on the Bay. Kieran cycles down there every day that it is sunny.

AT HOME
Kieran's home is built on land which belonged to Kieran's grandparents. There were once rows of greenhouses there, and although some were demolished to make way for the house, some derelict greenhouses are still standing.

Nigel grows many varieties of tomato, but he specializes in these small and deliciously sweet cherry tomatoes.

Kieran gets paid £2.50 for every crate he fills. With the money he earns, he buys things for his bike and for football.

THE VINERY
This glasshouse area is one of five belonging to Kieran's family. Glasshouses shelter tomato plants from bad weather so they bear fruit for a long time each year. Nigel once won an "Earliest Tomato" award when his plants bore fruit in February.

The glasshouse area is known as a vinery.

Tomatoes are picked when they have just turned red.

Each crate is three-quarters filled (with about 18 kilograms of tomatoes) to prevent tomatoes at the bottom from being squashed.

Nigel trims each tomato plant's sprouting leaves, leaving just the vine, so that all the plant's energies focus on producing fruit.

ORGANIC METHODS
Nigel grows his tomatoes organically. This means that he uses bees to fertilize his tomato plants, instead of using chemicals. He introduces insects that eat the bugs that are harmful to tomato plants, instead of using chemical pesticides.

FAMILY AT WORK
Teams of workers help trim and pick the tomato crop. In the summer, when each plant is laden with fruit, Kieran and his family also help with the picking.

KEEN FOOTBALLER
Kieran wants to be a professional footballer. He has made a football pitch in front of his house and he has been selected to play for the Guernsey Under 11s. Kieran really enjoyed watching the 1998 World Cup on television. His father videoed the England matches that took place when Kieran was at school, so Kieran could watch all the England games.

" I wouldn't want to live in a town where the houses are so close together. I think it's important to know how to use your hands, and not rely too much on computers. If computers go wrong in the future, people won't know what to do because they've forgotten how to work without them. "

HORSE RIDING
Behind Kieran's house is a field where Kieran and his sisters keep two ponies called Misty and Missy. Misty is Kieran's pony. He is 21 years old but still very good at jumping. Kieran takes him to horse shows all round the island.

Kieran won this shield in a jumping competition.

Kieran and Misty won this cup at a Pony Club show. They have won six others.

Kieran

Kieran supports Manchester United, but he has never seen them play. He was delighted when they won the FA Cup, the Premiership and the European Cup in 1999.

LOOKING BACK

1880s IN THE 19TH CENTURY, before Kieran was born, football in Britain was very different from today. Matches were not well organized, players were unpaid, there was little money involved in the game and there were no big clubs. Had Kieran been alive he would have supported a local team, rather than Manchester United. During the 1880s, football began to get more organized. Some players turned professional and tickets were issued for matches.

1884 Following an FA (Football Association) Cup match in 1884, this Preston team admitted to employing professional players. As a result, the Football League was established for professional teams. Preston North End were the first League champions.

1923 During the 1920s and 1930s local football teams were a source of pride. Fathers and sons flocked to games in their thousands after work on Saturdays. Big stadiums had to be built including Wembley Stadium which was finished in time for the 1923 FA Cup Final.

1966 In 1966, England won the World Cup for the first time in front of their own fans at Wembley Stadium. It was the proudest moment in the history of English football with England beating West Germany in the final 4-2.

Football may no longer be a local game but players come from every part of Britain. Matt Le Tissier comes from Kieran's home, Guernsey, and has fulfilled Kieran's dream of playing for England.

1970s Football began to be broadcast on television in the late 1960s, and became the most widely watched sport in the world. The 1970 World Cup was watched by over 40 million people worldwide. Kieran was one of the billions worldwide who watched the 1998 World Cup.

Young fans spend money on goods branded with their team's name, such as these replica shirts.

1990s Football is now a multi-million pound industry. Successful teams such as Manchester United have sold themselves on the stock exchange. Premiership clubs have negotiated their own television contracts with satellite channels such as Sky Sports; their players are national celebrities.

Samantha

"I'd like to go to Israel to meet lots of other Jewish people."

Samantha is 10 years old and lives in Leeds in Yorkshire. Her mother's family has lived in Leeds for many generations, but her father's family came from Poland. Samantha's family is Jewish. Samantha and her brother Charles, who is 14, are actively involved in the local Jewish community. They go to synagogue at least once a week and can read and write in Hebrew.

BALLOON BUSINESS
Samantha's mother runs her own business from home. She delivers gifts of balloons and organizes balloon displays for people's parties. Samantha often helps her mother put the finishing touches to displays in order to earn some extra pocket money.

Samantha loves roller-blading with her friends in the streets around her house. She also likes to go ice-skating.

BARMITZVAH
When a Jewish boy turns 13, he is allowed to sing a portion of the *Torah*, the Jewish Bible, in synagogue for the first time in a ceremony called a *Barmitzvah*. Charles spent months learning his portion and his family threw a big party to celebrate.

Samantha likes lots of authors. She particularly likes Judy Blume and thinks that every book by Roald Dahl is brilliant.

This is a photograph of Charles and his father taken during Charles's *Barmitzvah*.

SYNAGOGUE
Samantha and Charles walk to Shadwell Lane Synagogue for a service every week on *Shabbat*. They dress up smartly. Charles leads a service for children, telling jokes to make it fun. Samantha often helps look after the babies.

PRIVATE PLACE
Samantha's favourite place is her bedroom. The word "Samantha" is inlaid in pink in her carpet. She and Charles often fight because Samantha lets Charles in her bedroom, but Charles's room has a "no entry" sign.

The Zone is funded by the Leeds Jewish community.

Samantha goes to The Zone to play snooker with her friends every Wednesday.

The wine is *kosher*, meaning that it is made in accordance with strict Jewish laws about producing and eating food.

Candles are lit at many ceremonies.

Ceremonial wine is drunk from a *kiddush* cup.

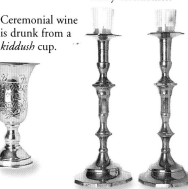

THE ZONE
Not far from Samantha's house is a youth club for Jewish children called The Zone, where Samantha and Charles meet their friends. There are lots of things to do, including table tennis, pool and video games. There are also discussions about what it means to be Jewish.

SHABBAT
The Jewish sabbath, called *Shabbat*, is from sundown on Friday night until sundown on Saturday. It is a day of rest from weekday work and worries. On Friday nights, Samantha's family share a *Shabbat* meal and say blessings over the food and wine. They eat chicken or fish, and plaited bread, called *Challah*.

Sophie is an eight-week-old Labrador puppy. Samantha has only had her for two weeks. Sophie is not allowed outside yet.

LOOKING BACK

1900 SAMANTHA IS PART OF A COMMUNITY that has existed in Britain for hundreds of years. At the end of the 19th century until 1950, thousands of European Jews emigrated to Britain to escape persecution abroad. Many of these were children sent by desperate parents or orphans whose families had been killed. They settled in the big cities where they arrived, such as London, Glasgow, Manchester and Liverpool. The community grew to number 300,000 people.

1930 Jewish refugees could not speak English and lived in cramped conditions in the worst parts of cities. Even those with good professions in their home countries ended up doing badly paid manual jobs. Many children worked sewing and mending in tailors' shops.

No matter where they were or what the conditions, families taught their children about their religion. At Passover every year, for example, families read how the Jews fled from Egypt in Biblical times.

1935 Despite hardships, many Jews prospered. A large number started their own businesses, like Samantha's mother did years later. In 1884, Russian refugee, Michael Marks, opened a market stall in Leeds. By 1935, he and a partner, Tom Spencer, had a string of shops selling "own brand" food and clothes. Their business grew rapidly into one of Britain's best-loved companies, Marks & Spencer.

A plate of ceremonial foods is used in the Passover festival.

A menorah is used during the festival of Hanukah and is a symbol of Judaism.

Tallis, or prayer shawl

A kippah is worn as a sign of respect for God.

The Jewish scriptures are written in Hebrew.

1948 British Jews celebrated the founding of the Jewish state of Israel in 1948. They felt that Jewish people now had somewhere to go if they were persecuted in their own countries.

Samantha

"I wish people would stop judging other people by their skin colour. I wish that scientists would stop testing things on animals first, because they are living things. Most of all I would like to stop all the fighting and that there would be no bad people in the world. It would be nice if the world had no gravity and you were just floating in the air like a balloon. You could fly!"

שָׂרָה לֵאָה

Samantha has a Hebrew name, Sarah Leah. She has written it in Hebrew script. It reads from right to left.

Francesca

"My wish is to be able to walk just a little way."

Francesca is 12 years old and lives on Canvey Island in Essex with her mother, father and brother. Francesca has cerebral palsy. This is not a disease or an illness, but a physical condition that leaves muscles hard to control, making it difficult to talk or to move around by yourself.

Francesca made this picture on her computer for her school homework.

TOY MAD
Francesca's bedroom is filled with hundreds of toys. She has dolls, teddy bears and other soft toys crammed from wall to wall. Francesca has kept every toy that has ever been given to her, and she has a special place for each one. Her favourite toy is her new doll, who has no name.

Francesca likes to play board games and computer games with eight-year-old Daniel.

WAY WITH WORDS
This laptop computer has a voice which tells Francesca which key she has typed. She uses it for homework and for writing stories. Francesca would need help to write by hand. Her computer allows her to express herself through written words on her own.

Joystick allows Francesca to control the cursor on the screen.

SOAP QUEEN
The TV is often on at Francesca's home. She loves soap operas, especially *EastEnders*. Francesca always plays with her brother, Daniel. He has no disabilities and is very helpful to his sister.

Francesca has programmed one of the symbols to represent her brother, Daniel.

TIME TO CHAT
This Delta Talker computer is used by people who cannot talk easily to communicate. Each key represents a word, which Francesca can program to be whatever she likes. She can then type sentences rapidly which appear on the screen. She can also use the voice synthesizer which says the word that is pressed, so she can use the Talker to chat.

Francesca often listens to music and her favourite groups are Boyzone and Steps. Her brother likes them too and they have lots of their tapes.

Scary tales and fairy stories are what Francesca likes to read and write most. She has read lots of *Goosebumps* books from the famous horror series.

Recently, Francesca stayed away from home for the very first time when she went on a school trip.

She loves playing on the beach on holiday as the sand is so soft and warm.

SWIMMING
Francesca cannot walk on her own. She loves swimming as the water takes the weight from her limbs and allows her to float unaided. She particularly enjoys ducking her head beneath the water.

Francesca bought jodhpurs with her birthday money.

ON HORSEBACK
Once a week, Francesca has horse riding lessons on a pony called Pebbles, who is very obedient. Her riding instructor is from the RDA, the Riding for the Disabled Association. She is taught the basics of a good riding posture: how to sit, hold the reins and keep her feet in the stirrups. She has to use a lot of concentration and effort but riding helps to improve her co-ordination.

Francesca uses this buggy when her mother needs to go shopping or when she has to go too far to be carried.

"The only thing I don't like is getting up early in the morning before school. I always like to get up slowly and have coffee in bed with my mum before doing anything."

LOOKING BACK

1900 AT THE TURN OF THE CENTURY, most of the half a million people in Britain with disabilities were children. Their families got little help except from charities. Hundreds of thousands of children ended up living in institutions because their families could not afford the care they needed. Many who stayed at home didn't go to school, because schools did not have to cater for pupils with special needs. Without education, it was hard to get a job when they grew up.

For ten years, computer technology has helped children with disabilities to learn at school.

1939 When World War II broke out, millions of men became soldiers. People with disabilities took their places at work, doing jobs such as managing factories and nursing. But when the war ended, they were pushed back into low-paid, unskilled work.

Charities still help those with disabilities – these children are on a holiday organized by Scope.

1940s A series of laws from the 1940s set up a national health and education service. People with disabilities could now get education and health care for free. Experts such as social workers and occupational therapists were trained to help them. It is now very rare for children with disabilities to live in institutions – the majority are catered for in ordinary schools.

LEARNING
Francesca goes to a school for children with disabilities. There are seven children in her class. She uses an automatic wheelchair at school that she can operate herself. Three times a year, she goes to "Peto Andras Conductive Education" classes. Here she learns how to control her body better.

When I am older I'd like to look after young children and babies. I love babies, but I wouldn't like to have any of my own. I wouldn't want to go through the pregnancy and having them. If I could change the world, I wish I could change all the natural disasters and wars that affect other people.

BIG BIKE
Francesca can ride her tricycle unaided. The pedals have special braces and the seat has a belt which goes round her waist to protect her from falling off, if her limbs move without her wanting them to.

Inderjivan

HOME ON TOP
Inderjivan's mother came to England from India when she was a girl. His father, Harjivan, came in 1985, and then met and married his mother. They own a newsagent's shop and a kiosk at a metro station. They live above their shop. Everybody calls Harjivan "Harry", and his shop, "Harry's Shop".

"The best thing about having a sweet shop is all the ice cream I get."

Inderjivan is 11 years old and lives in Newcastle. His parents were originally from India, but Inderjivan and his sisters were born in England. Inderjivan wears a turban over his head because he is Sikh. Sikhism is a religion that began 500 years ago in the Punjab in northern India.

These brightly coloured cloth squares are called *patkas*. Inderjivan wears one on his head every day.

A portrait of Guru Nanak, who founded Sikhism in the 1400s.

CHESS MATCH
Inderjivan is very close to his two sisters and has taught the eldest to play chess. The younger sister annoys them while they play, so they sometimes play Monopoly with her.

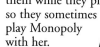

The Beano is Inderjivan's favourite comic.

SHELF FILLER
After school, Inderjivan often helps his father in the newsagent's. He tidies up the stockroom, or checks what is running low on the shelves and fills them up. He also helps on the till.

SUNDAY LUNCH
Inderjivan's family mostly eat Italian food, like pizzas or pasta. For Sunday lunch, they enjoy a traditional Sikh vegetarian meal of *dahl* (lentils) and *subzi* (vegetables). Sharing a meal is important in Sikh culture. Free vegetarian meals are always on offer at Sikh temples.

LOOKING BACK

1940s AFTER WORLD WAR II ended in 1945, workers were needed in Britain to rebuild bomb-damaged cities. As the economy recovered, they were also needed in transport, the newly created National Health Service and manufacturing industries. The government encouraged men to emigrate from current and former British colonies in Africa, the Caribbean and Asia. Thousands of immigrants from India were Sikhs.

1950s In India, Sikhs were well educated and used to taking part in national life. Inderjivan's grandfather was active in the Indian student movement, and is shown here in 1947 with Indian leader, Mahatma Gandhi. In Britain, Sikhs could often only find badly paid jobs in textile mills, foundries and factories.

Inderjivan's grandfather

1970s The children of Sikh immigrants grew up in Britain speaking English as well as Punjabi. They were confident enough to start their own businesses, ranging from restaurants to clothing companies. Harjivan followed this trend.

By the 1970s, laws stopped Asians coming to Britain unless they were at risk in their home countries, or if they married someone living in Britain, like Harjivan (right) did.

The holiest place in the world for Sikhs is the Golden Temple in the Punjab. Sikh people follow the teaching of Guru Nanak, who believed that there is one God. People should form a relationship with God with the help of a guru (spiritual guide).

Sikh immigrants moved into cities such as London, Manchester, Sheffield, Bradford and Newcastle, where there were most jobs.

Kamani   Tamana

Inderjivan

"*I've been to India three times. It was really good. I'd like to live in Bombay or Calcutta because my dad's got relatives there and it's really nice. The only thing that spooked me out was a tarantula in the house. If I could change anything in the world, I would want to wipe out nuclear and atomic bombs, because they would be bad for my chest.*"

"*Dad went in April of last year to Calcutta and he bought me the* tabla."

PUTTING ON A PATKA
Sikh men do not cut their hair and keep it covered. Inderjivan's hair used to reach his ankles, but because of damage from chemicals such as chlorine it now only reaches his knees. People cannot see how long Inderjivan's hair is because it is always tied in a bun and covered in a *patka* to keep it in place. A *patka* is a kind of turban, a piece of cloth five metres long.

It takes Inderjivan about half an hour to put on a *patka*, including the time it takes to comb his hair before he starts.

This hammer is used to tune the small drum called the *Dayan*. The tuner taps the rim with the hammer, then tightens and taps the pad until the sounds chime.

Inderjivan changes his *patka* every day.

SISTERS
Inderjivan has two younger sisters, Tamana and Kamani. Tamana means "heart's desire", Kamani means "fragrant flower" and Inderjivan means "water of life" in Punjabi. Most Sikh boys have the middle name *Singh*, meaning "lion", and girls have the middle name *Kaur*, meaning "princess".

Inderjivan is called "Indy" for short by his friends and teachers at school.

BEAT MUSIC
Each drum beat is written as a different syllable, rather than a note. Inderjivan memorises the syllables and sings them aloud while making the right drum beat.

Talcum powder

Talcum powder is sprinkled on the drums to protect them from the drummer's sweaty hands.

DRUM BEAT
Inderjivan plays the piano and Indian drums called *tabla*. He accompanies classical Indian music on his *tabla* every Saturday with a group called Gurul Kul. It has 60 musicians, who play the *sitar* (a sort of Indian guitar), harmonica, the *tabla* and sing. A teacher comes from Delhi, India's capital, every six months to teach them.

Douglas

"When I grow up, I'd like to be a farmer like my dad."

Douglas is 10 years old and lives on a small farm in Berkshire. Douglas's father manages the farm, which is mainly a sheep farm. Every day, Douglas has chores to do as farm life is always busy. Animals must be fed, crops planted and land must be looked after.

HELPING ON THE FARM
When Douglas is not at school, he helps his father with important jobs, such as preparing the land for sheep to graze. They divide off a section of a field with an electric fence. The sheep graze this section for six days, then another section is prepared for them. This way none of the grass is eaten down to the ground.

TREE HOUSE
Douglas made this tree house with his 12-year-old sister, Polly. They cut the pieces of wood themselves.

FARMHOUSE
Douglas, his sister Polly, his dad and Sandy, his dad's partner, live here. Polly and Douglas stay with their mum every other weekend.

When Douglas is out and about on the farm, he wears a waterproof coat to protect him from the rain. The coat is treated with wax, so water just slides off its surface.

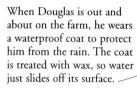

" Meg is my favourite dog because she is so cuddly. But she only listens to what my father tells her to do."

Douglas's father only has to whistle or shout a few commands, and his sheepdogs will round up any number of sheep. The sheep may then be sheared, checked over or moved on to new grazing.

FEEDING MEG
Every day, it is Douglas's job to feed the dogs. The farm has three sheepdogs and two pet Labradors. The sheepdogs are called Meg, Sweep and Moss. They are Border Collies. Collies are good farm dogs as they are obedient, intelligent and easily trained to round up sheep. Sometimes the sheepdogs on Douglas's farm round up the chickens as well!

FEEDING THE GEESE
Geese, chickens and ducks are kept on Douglas's farm for their eggs. At night, the birds are shut away in the barn to protect them from being eaten by foxes. When Douglas "puts them to bed" the geese are sometimes naughty and refuse to go. Once Douglas was pecked on the leg. He offers the geese snacks to coax them into the barn.

EGG COLLECTING
Douglas's sister, Polly, checks the barn every morning to see whether any of the birds have laid eggs. Douglas hunts for eggs which have been laid in unusual places, such as under the tractors.

" My dad lets me help him do most things on the farm. I help him to check the sheep in the fields a lot. Sometimes we go there on the 'Quad' bike, or we go by tractor. When I grow up, I would like to be a farmer like my dad. I would work with sheep and cattle, just like my dad does. "

Douglas

HUNTING RABBITS
Douglas likes hunting for rabbits with his father. The number of rabbits must be controlled to stop them damaging the crops. Douglas's father shoots the rabbits. He sometimes skins and cooks the rabbits, and the family eat them for supper.

PET FERRETS
Douglas has two ferrets. One is called Nasty and the other is called Tickles because he runs all over Douglas and tickles him behind the ears. Douglas made a ferret run from old pieces of wood and some chicken wire.

GETTING AROUND
Douglas drives around the farm with his father in the tractor or on the "Quad" – a motorbike with four wheels. They fix attachments to the back of the tractor so it can be used for ploughing, sowing and drilling.

LOOKING BACK

1890s In late Victorian times, farm children, like Douglas, went out into the fields with their fathers. Everyone was expected to lend a hand with the harvest. The workers cut and raked the hay, then loaded it onto hay carts by hand. There were jobs for children at other times of the year, too. In the spring, young boys often worked as scarecrows! They made a noise by clapping two boards together, rattling stones in a tin, or shouting to scare the birds away from the crops.

Hay cart

Hay loader

1900 Country children were needed to help on the farm, feeding the geese and chickens, and milking the cows. They often only went to school part-time, or left school before the age of 10.

In the past, many workers were needed to do the jobs now done by machinery. On Douglas's farm, hay is collected and stacked by a tractor and baler.

Sara Lee

Eleven-year-old Sara Lee is a gypsy, who lives with her family in two trailers. When there is a family gathering or a gypsy fair to go to, Sara Lee, her parents and sisters pack everything away and move to wherever it is taking place. They find a school for Sara Lee and her sisters to attend. At the moment the family live in Oxfordshire, on a caravan site.

"I never want to live in a house."

MOTHER AND FATHER'S TRAILER
Sara Lee's family own two trailers and a truck to tow them. Finding a place to stop can be hard. Many old gypsy stopping places have been built on or fenced off, and many gypsies end up on caravan sites. There are 20 gypsy families on Sara Lee's site, so it is like a village. The site provides water and electricity.

INSIDE THE TRAILER
Sara Lee's parents recently bought this trailer. It is the 11th trailer they have owned. They liked it because it has a particularly comfortable bed. Rosie girl, Sara Lee's six-year-old sister, sleeps in this trailer, on a fold-out bed. The trailer has a TV, video and stereo. The family also have a mobile phone.

"On my first day at one school, the chairs and tables were so dirty, I cleaned them before I sat down."

SARA Lee

"I love living in a trailer. I would never want to live in a house. Whenever we want to move on, we don't have to sell our home, we just pack up and off we go. When we pack things like the china or our toys, we clean them until they shine like gold. When I grow up, I would like to eat off paper plates and drink out of plastic cups so there is no washing up! Most of all I hope that people will leave us alone and treat us with respect, just like everybody else.

Jill is a puppy that the family has just found.

SUPERSTITIONS
Gypsies have many traditional sayings about good and bad fortune. For example, if you buy a broom in the month of May, you could brush your family away. Also in May, it's bad luck to cut your hair.

Jack is the family's favourite dog.

SARA LEE'S TRAILER

Sara Lee and her nine-year-old sister, Colleen, sleep in their own trailer. All three sisters are lying on the biggest bed, which belongs to Sara Lee. This is one of Sara Lee's privileges as the eldest sister, but she also has the responsibility of looking after her siblings. The girls love singing. Often the whole family sings together and Sara Lee's father plays the accordion.

Jacks is one of the sisters' favourite games. They also like playing leapfrog and hide-and-seek around the caravan site.

BATHTIME

The three sisters have baths in the traditional gypsy way, which has changed very little in the last century. They collect water in churns and cans and heat it to a warm temperature. Then they pour the water into a steel bath tub and take it in turns to have a bath.

Stainless steel churn, can and bath are kept outside the door of the trailer.

Steel can with spout for pouring hot water into the bath

Steel bath is big enough for Sara Lee to sit in, but not lie in.

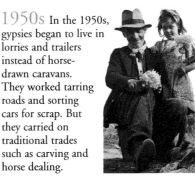

HORSE FAIR

Gypsies trade their horses, buy special goods and meet up with friends and relatives at large annual fairs. Sara Lee's family bought their three horses, Queenie, Gypsy and Andrew at fairs. Sara Lee's job is to ride on a horse as it is being shown to prospective buyers. Her father did the same when he was a boy.

HEIRLOOMS

These gold bracelets and rings were given to Sara Lee by her parents. Her favourite piece is the gold chain with the Krugerrand (South African coin) pendant. It belonged to her great-grandmother and is over 100 years old.

Krugerrand

"The best place I think we've ever lived, is where my nanny lives in Wraysbury. I like it there because there are lots of dogs that I can stroke."

PRECIOUS PATTERN

Traditionally, gypsies collect a type of china made in the last century called Crown Derby. This plate is one of the family's many pieces of Crown Derby. Whenever they travel, they wrap their china in towels so that nothing breaks.

LOOKING BACK

1800s GYPSIES PROBABLY originated in India 1,000 years ago and made their way overland to Europe. They came to England in about 1500 and from that time travelled around the country trading and hiring themselves out to do farm work. In about 1830, they moved from tents to "vardos" – wooden horse-drawn caravans.

1950s In the 1950s, gypsies began to live in lorries and trailers instead of horse-drawn caravans. They worked tarring roads and sorting cars for scrap. But they carried on traditional trades such as carving and horse dealing.

Sara Lee's great-grandparents lived in a caravan like this one. The design was adapted from farm carts and railway carriages. Caravans were beautifully painted and decorated.

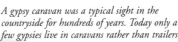

A gypsy caravan was a typical sight in the countryside for hundreds of years. Today only a few gypsies live in caravans rather than trailers.

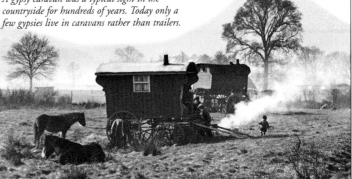

Carl fights world tae kwon-do champion, Mark Ogborne

Carl

"I'm the youngest black belt in the country."

Ten-year-old Carl from Exeter is one of the top young tae kwon-do fighters in the country. Tae kwon-do is a Korean martial art, which Carl practises as a fitness sport. Carl's father takes time off his job at the local paper to take him to tournaments, and Carl often appears in the paper to celebrate his achievements.

PRACTICE MAKES PERFECT
Carl first joined a tae kwon-do class at his local sports' centre five years ago. "Tae kwon-do" means "the way of the foot and fist" in Korean. Carl uses his legs and arms to defeat an opponent in combat.

TRAINING
At tae kwon-do class, Carl practises sequences of attack and defence movements on his own and spars with an opponent to develop these skills in action. He also practises breaks – splitting wood with a powerful kick.

Fighters wear padded helmets while sparring.

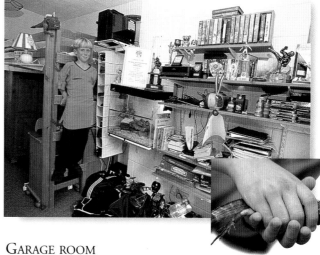

Mitts protect Carl's knuckles.

WINNER
At tournaments, Carl fights an opponent for two or three two-minute rounds on a padded mat. The judge awards points for kicks or punches, and the opponent with the most points wins. Carl can also win awards for breaks and for performing patterns of movements the best.

Trainers protect Carl's opponent from bruises when Carl kicks.

GARAGE ROOM
Carl's parents converted their garage into a bedroom for Carl big enough to practise tae kwon-do in. Carl likes his new room because he has so much more space, peace and quiet.

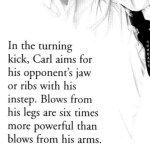

Carl's lizard, Spot

Carl and his father keep lizards. They feed them dead moths, crickets and worms every day, which they buy from a pet shop or catch.

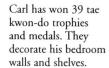

Carl has won 39 tae kwon-do trophies and medals. They decorate his bedroom walls and shelves.

RAW POWER
Carl is progressing through the tae kwon-do grades. To achieve each new grade he has to demonstrate an increasingly difficult pattern of movements and spar in front of a tae kwon-do master. He practises at home to improve his muscular power, flexibility and readiness.

Blocks

Carl uses blocks to defend himself from punches or kicks.

Carl uses his forearms and shins in blocking.

Strike

This strike is called an upper cut elbow strike. Carl brings his right hand over his shoulder so he doesn't punch his own face.

Carl always trains barefoot, unless he's sparring.

Kick

In the turning kick, Carl aims for his opponent's jaw or ribs with his instep. Blows from his legs are six times more powerful than blows from his arms.

During the side kick, Carl leans his head and upper body away from an opponent to keep clear of them.

"Tae kwon-do is very hard work, but I still love it. Most people think that black belt is the highest you can go, but I still have nine more dans before I'm at the very top."

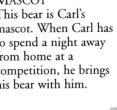

MASCOT
This bear is Carl's mascot. When Carl has to spend a night away from home at a competition, he brings his bear with him.

BELTS
There are 10 basic grades in tae kwon-do. Fighters get one of five coloured belts or a tag for that belt as they progress. At black belt, the highest belt stage, the gradings are called dans. The best possible tae kwon-do grade is the tenth dan.

CERTIFICATE
To get his black belt, Carl had to show mental and physical discipline. He had to do 13 patterns and learn the names of the movements in Korean.

To do a side kick, Carl brings his left foot behind his right foot and lifts his right knee. Then he thrusts his right heel horizontally into his opponent's body.

Carl wears the traditional cotton tae kwon-do suit.

Carl

I like doing tae kwon-do. It keeps me healthy and I'll be able to look after myself. When I grow up, I'd like to be a professional footballer, but if not, I could be a tae kwon-do instructor. The only thing I don't like in the world is the horrible things like stealing and fighting.

MEDIA STAR
Carl has two scrapbooks full of newspaper cuttings about his triumphs. He has been photographed and interviewed many times, including by his father's newspaper, the *Exeter Express and Echo*.

LOOKING BACK

1904 THE EXETER EXPRESS AND ECHO was founded in 1904, 80 years before Carl's father began work there. Before this time, there were a few, very serious newspapers such as *The Times*. In 1903, Lord Northcliffe launched a "tabloid", *The Daily Mirror*. Half the size of a standard paper, it contained sensational stories and features. At the same time, tabloid-sized papers sprung up all over the country to cover different regions. From the beginning, local papers reported on the special achievements of local children.

The Daily Mirror *reports the sinking of the Titanic in 1912.*

In the early 19th century, newspaper production was slow. Every letter was a separate metal letter put in a wooden tray to make up a page. Now production managers, like Carl's father, create pages on computers, which are sent electronically to printing presses.

Helene

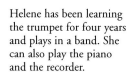

"I like living in Manchester. It rains a lot. I like the rain."

Helene is ten years old and lives in Manchester. She and her brothers were born in England. Her parents were born in the Caribbean, a string of islands off central America, but came to live in England when they were young. Every year, Helene and her family go on holiday to the Caribbean to visit friends and relatives.

Helene has been learning the trumpet for four years and plays in a band. She can also play the piano and the recorder.

PLENTY OF ROOM
At home, Helene and her brothers, Simon (7) and Andrew (14), each have their own bedroom. Their mother is a lawyer and their father is a psychologist. They both work very hard, so they are not at home much during the week.

JERK CHICKEN
On Saturdays, when the whole family is together, they share a meal. Sometimes Helene's father cooks a dish from the Caribbean, jerk chicken. He was born on the Caribbean island of Trinidad.

Jerk is a spicy, seasoned paste made from chillies, onions, salt and pepper. It is spread over the chicken, which is then grilled.

TREASURE BOX
This painted wooden box, which looks like a leather-bound book, is Helene's secret treasure box. It was a gift from her mother. Its contents are so secret that only her brother Simon has been allowed to look inside it, once.

After spreading jerk chicken paste, Helene washes the paste off her hands, or the chillies may burn.

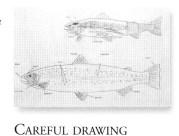

ALL THAT JAZZ
Helene wears red shoes to tap dancing lessons once a week. They have steel under the toes which taps when she brushes the floor. She has taken three tap dancing grades and got these trophies (left) for passing them. Helene also learns ballet, but thinks it is harder than tap.

2PAC
Helene's hamster is called 2Pac because his cheeks look like two pockets, or packs. He is also named after Rap artist Tupac Shakur (2Pac).

After a fight with a family cat, the vet saved 2Pac's life. But 2Pac is now blind in one eye.

CAREFUL DRAWING
Helene drew and labelled some fish for a school science project. Science is her best subject. She enjoys learning about the features of different animals and wants to be a biologist when she grows up.

HAIR STYLE
Plaiting hair tight and close to the scalp is a traditional Caribbean and African style called cornrowing. Helene wears her hair in the cornrowing style, canerow. It looks like the neat rows of corn and sugarcane grown back in the Caribbean. Helene's mother may plait Helene's hair, but the hairdresser can do it in 30 minutes. The same plait can stay in for two weeks. Helene sleeps with a scarf over her hair to prevent the plaits coming undone.

RIVER MERSEY
At the end of Helene's street is the River Mersey, which flows all the way to Liverpool from Manchester. Helene cycles along the winding riverbank.

Simon looks up to Helene.

"I like playing the trumpet. When Simon and I argue, then I just blow it really hard so I can't hear him."

❝ *It's nice on holiday in Trinidad. I like seeing my family, going to the beach and exploring the forest where there are loads of snakes. It rains every morning and I just sit there and listen. It sounds really nice and soothing. When I grow up, I'd like to be a biologist. I would learn all about the body and find new cures for diseases like cancer and AIDS. In the future, I think there will be flying cars. I'd like to live in London. It's a bit busy there but I like busy places.* ❞

Helene

"Both my brothers tease me. I sort of like it, though. I don't know why."

Andrew   Simon   Helene

HOLIDAY SNAP
Helene's family go on holiday to Trinidad, or to a smaller Caribbean island, Nevis, where her mother was born. Helene loves the hot, sandy beaches and lush forests, though there are mosquitoes that may bite. She eats a lot of fresh fruit and fish such as swordfish. She has been to carnival in Trinidad twice.

LOOKING BACK

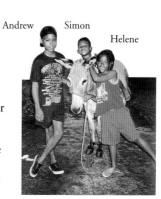

Helene's whistle for carnival in Trinidad

1950s HELENE AND HER FAMILY are part of the black community, which has existed in Britain since the 17th century. The community grew rapidly after World War II, when the government asked people from British colonies in Africa and the Caribbean to move to Britain to work. Many black people found life in Britain tough. They were often paid worse than white people and found it hard to find housing.

1976 The government introduced some laws to protect black people. The 1976 Race Relations Act made it illegal to discriminate against anyone on grounds of race, colour, nationality or ethnic origin.

1970s Caribbean people brought traditions such as carnival with them. Carnival is a celebration of freedom. The first Notting Hill Carnival in London was held in 1958. By the 1970s, it was one of Europe's biggest festivals.

1950–90s Black culture became a vital part of British culture. Black churchgoers breathed new life into the Christian church. British people became familiar with Caribbean music such as reggae and could buy and cook Caribbean food.

Sugar cane

Okra   Mangoes   Green bananas   Yam   Dasheen   Bread fruit   Plantain

Papaya   Sweet potato   Chow   Cassava

Blogo

Binita

"I don't have any brothers or sisters or pets, so I see my friends after school."

Twelve-year-old Binita lives on top of a shop. Her parents are from Kenya; her grandparents were from India. She speaks English and Gujerati, an Indian dialect, at home.

" In the millennium, I want to do very well at school and get good exam results. I also want to stop poverty, so that everyone in the world can be happy. "

Binita

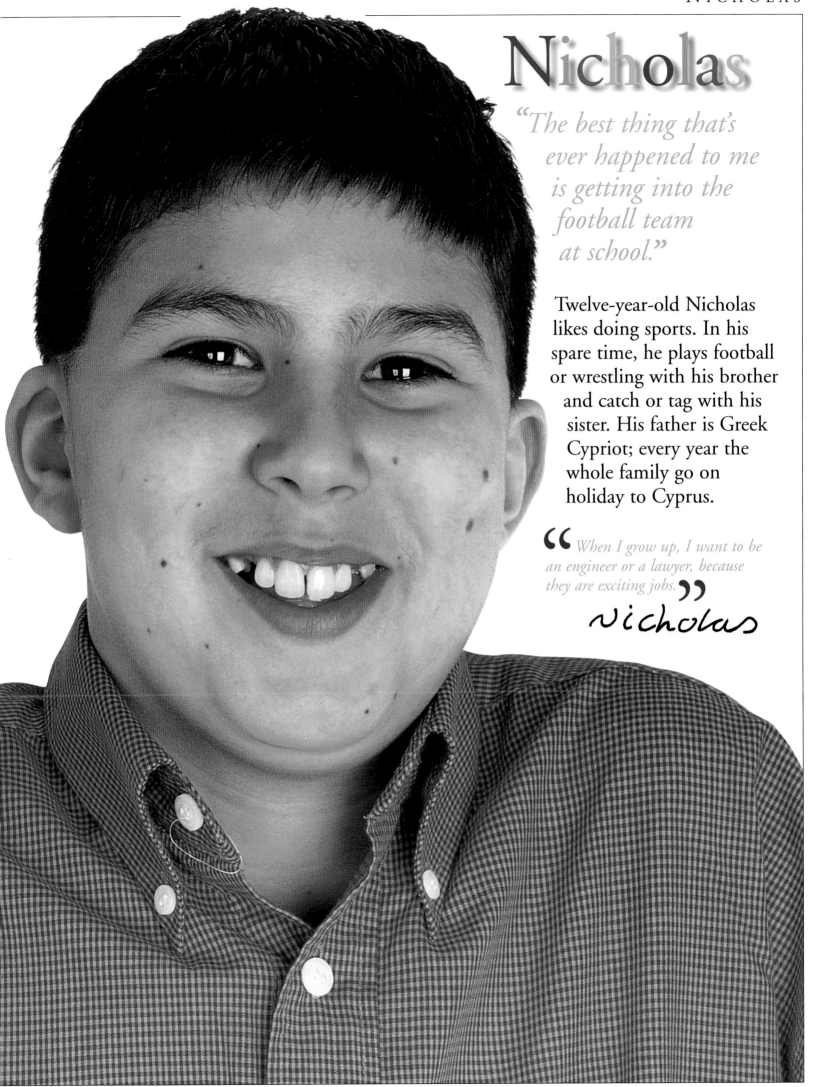

Nicholas

"The best thing that's ever happened to me is getting into the football team at school."

Twelve-year-old Nicholas likes doing sports. In his spare time, he plays football or wrestling with his brother and catch or tag with his sister. His father is Greek Cypriot; every year the whole family go on holiday to Cyprus.

" When I grow up, I want to be an engineer or a lawyer, because they are exciting jobs. "

Nicholas

FAMILY HOME
Phillip's house is down a small country lane outside a village called Pontarddulais, which means "bridge over the river Dulais" in Welsh. Phillip and his 14-year-old brother, Gareth, have lived in the house since they were born.

Local map

Worksheets give useful advice on outdoor activities.

Scouts learn to use a compass.

MAP READING
One basic skill that a scout must learn is how to read a map. Troops of scouts are divided into sets of six, called patrols. Gareth is the leader of Phillip's patrol. When the patrol goes out map reading, Gareth helps the others to identify map symbols, such as churches and bridges.

GOOD COOK
Scouts learn many different activities, from computing to car mechanics to cookery. Phillip has learnt to cook many dishes on "cookery night". He can make spaghetti bolognaise, cheese on toast, and his best dish, an omelette.

Phillip practises on his brother's cello.

MAKING MUSIC
Phillip has been learning to play the cello for four years. He has lessons once a week and plays in his school orchestra. Practising is hard work, but Phillip knows he must practise regularly to improve.

Phillip

"I'm learning how to survive in the wild."

Phillip's model aeroplane – he wants to be a pilot when he is older.

Eleven-year-old Phillip is from South Wales. He lives in a village not far from Swansea. Phillip is a scout. Scout troops for boys aged 11 and over, and Guide companies for girls aged 10 and over, were set up in the early 20th century to involve children in outdoor activities. Scouts are encouraged to be useful citizens and to do a good deed every day. At Scouts, Phillip learns skills to survive in the wild that are also useful in everyday life.

LOOKING BACK

1908 THE FIRST SCOUTS were 20 boys who went to camp on Brownsea Island, off Dorset, in 1907. Their leader, Baden-Powell, was a Major-General in the British army and taught the boys the skills that cavalry officers used in scouting (information gathering), such as how to follow tracks, read maps and signal. The camp was a great success, and Baden-Powell founded the scout movement in 1908. Soon there were scouts all over the country.

Baden-Powell fought in the Boer War between Britain and the South African Boers (1899-1902).

Lord Baden-Powell (1857-1941)

Scouts have always saluted with their right hands and shaken hands with their left hands.

This guide was published in 1908.

1925 Scouting quickly spread abroad. The first jamboree, held in 1920, was attended by scouts from 34 countries. Scout troops were often linked to churches, schools and community groups – above is a Leeds school troop photographed in 1925.

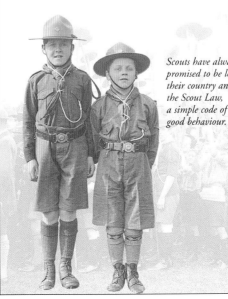

Scouts have always promised to be loyal to their country and obey the Scout Law, a simple code of good behaviour.

Phillip records his scouting achievements in this book.

Today, there are more than one million scouts and Guides in the UK. Phillip's troop is one of hundreds nationwide.

1925 Lots of girls were interested in the scouting movement. In 1910, Baden-Powell and his sister, Agnes, founded the Girl Guides to train girls in citizenship, good conduct and outdoor activities. This 1925 picture shows Guides and scouts saluting Baden-Powell, by this time called "Chief Scout of the World".

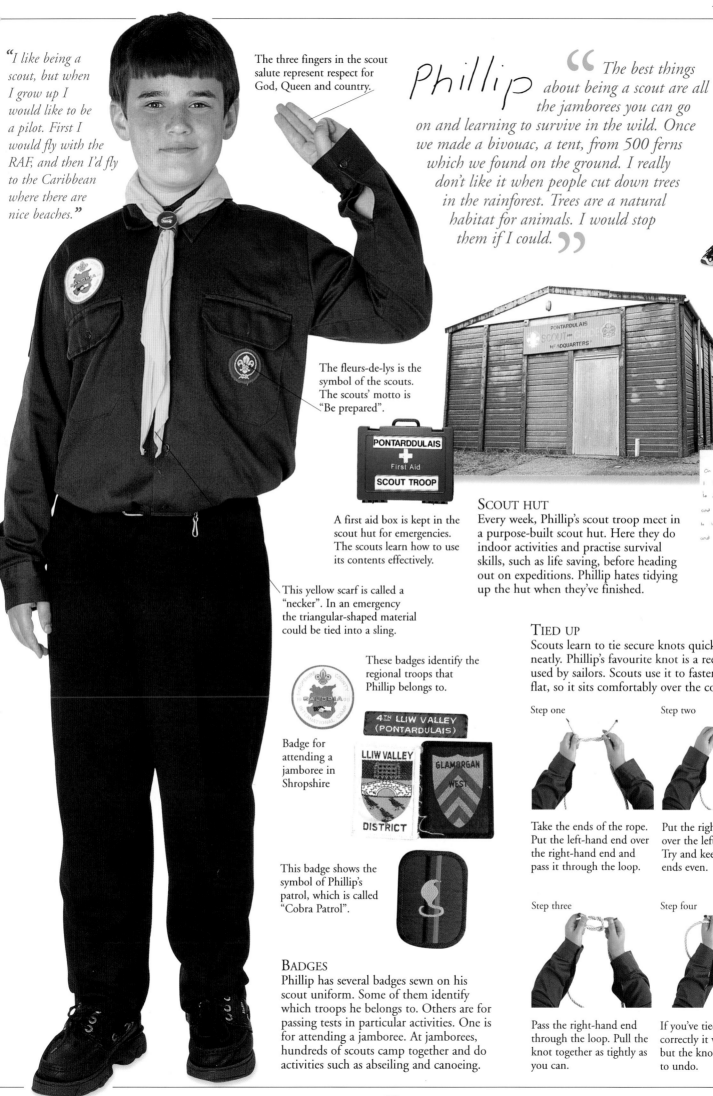

"I like being a scout, but when I grow up I would like to be a pilot. First I would fly with the RAF, and then I'd fly to the Caribbean where there are nice beaches."

The three fingers in the scout salute represent respect for God, Queen and country.

Phillip

" The best things about being a scout are all the jamborees you can go on and learning to survive in the wild. Once we made a bivouac, a tent, from 500 ferns which we found on the ground. I really don't like it when people cut down trees in the rainforest. Trees are a natural habitat for animals. I would stop them if I could. "

The fleurs-de-lys is the symbol of the scouts. The scouts' motto is "Be prepared".

A first aid box is kept in the scout hut for emergencies. The scouts learn how to use its contents effectively.

SCOUT HUT
Every week, Phillip's scout troop meet in a purpose-built scout hut. Here they do indoor activities and practise survival skills, such as life saving, before heading out on expeditions. Phillip hates tidying up the hut when they've finished.

Phillip has written out the scout promise.

This yellow scarf is called a "necker". In an emergency the triangular-shaped material could be tied into a sling.

These badges identify the regional troops that Phillip belongs to.

Badge for attending a jamboree in Shropshire

4TH LLIW VALLEY (PONTARDULAIS)

LLIW VALLEY DISTRICT

GLAMORGAN WEST

This badge shows the symbol of Phillip's patrol, which is called "Cobra Patrol".

BADGES
Phillip has several badges sewn on his scout uniform. Some of them identify which troops he belongs to. Others are for passing tests in particular activities. One is for attending a jamboree. At jamborees, hundreds of scouts camp together and do activities such as abseiling and canoeing.

TIED UP
Scouts learn to tie secure knots quickly and neatly. Phillip's favourite knot is a reef knot, often used by sailors. Scouts use it to fasten a sling. It is flat, so it sits comfortably over the collarbone.

Step one

Take the ends of the rope. Put the left-hand end over the right-hand end and pass it through the loop.

Step two

Put the right-hand end over the left-hand end. Try and keep the two ends even.

Step three

Pass the right-hand end through the loop. Pull the knot together as tightly as you can.

Step four

If you've tied the knot correctly it will not slip, but the knot will be easy to undo.

Alice

"My daddy's a vet and we've got seven animals and some fish."

Alice and Stuart live in the country near the town of Ipswich in Suffolk. They love living in their house because it's a big house with a big garden where they can play their favourite ball games such as tennis and football.

Alice is eight years old and lives in East Anglia. Her parents own a veterinary practice, where her father treats ill pets and farm animals. Alice's home is next to the surgery. Alice and her elder brother, Stuart, often visit the poorly patients that stay overnight in the kennels.

CONVERSION
Two old barns were converted into the surgery and Alice's home. Alice's living room is an open space with high ceilings and wooden beams, which would have been the central part of one barn. Alice's bedroom was probably a tool room.

Toothbrush

Stethoscope

Syringe for injecting horses

Cat and dog syringe

HARD WORK
Alice sweeps and mops the floors in the surgery, and helps clean out the kennels and spray them with disinfectant. If a dog has problems having puppies, Alice and Stuart may hold newborn puppies to keep them warm. No sick animal has ever bitten her.

VETS IN PRACTICE
Alice's father, Robert, works at the Barn Veterinary Surgery. Her mother is the surgery manager, who does the administration. As well as performing operations, Robert gives animals injections to protect them from disease, checks their hearts, and cleans their teeth if they have bad breath!

Barn Veterinary Surgery

The vets treat cats, horses, dogs, birds, chickens, geese, guinea pigs, hamsters and rabbits. After an operation, some animals need to stay overnight in kennels.

Here Robert is performing a minor operation to remove a lump from a Labrador's paw.

Alice's favourite subject is Art – she traced this horse.

HORSEWOMAN
Alice has been learning to ride for a year. Unfortunately, the family pony, Daisy, is too small to be ridden. So for the holidays, Alice is borrowing a pony called Robin from a friend. She rides Robin every day.

Robin is a chestnut-coloured Shetland pony.

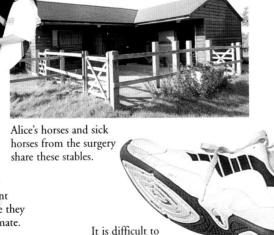

Alice's horses and sick horses from the surgery share these stables.

A surgery client gave this beautiful Siamese cat to Alice. She is called Chloe.

Ostriches make a change from the usual animals at the surgery, but they have been known to kick!

Iguanas are popular pets, but they need careful handling, and constant monitoring of their health because they are not naturally suited to our climate.

It is difficult to decide what is wrong with a tortoise.

Small, furry pets such as hamsters are becoming very popular. They are common visitors to the surgery.

ADOPTING PETS

Alice's family have one horse, two dogs, three cats, some fish and a parrot called Stanley. Most of these animals came from the surgery. Some were unwanted or badly treated. This picture is of Alice and Stuart with Skipper.

Sam's original owner thought he was vicious and wanted to put him down but Robert thought Sam was lovely and offered to give him a home. Sam is Skipper's dad.

Once, when a dog was having babies, she had to have an operation, and me and my brother had to keep the new-born puppies warm by rubbing them. One puppy was so small its eyes were closed. I don't want to be a vet. You have to do yukky things and get your hands yukky. I think it's sad when animals die. I'd like to teach people to ride.

Alice

HORSE BOOKS

When she's not mopping the floor in the surgery, feeding the animals or riding Robin, Alice reads horse books. These are two of her favourites.

"Every morning I get up and feed the horses apples and carrots. They have to have a proper feed, too."

Stuart is Alice's 10-year-old brother.

LOOKING BACK

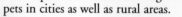

1950s IF ALICE'S FATHER had been a vet 100 years ago, he would have worked in a country village examining farm animals such as sheep, cows and horses. It was only in the 1950s and 1960s that vets started to spend more time treating domestic pets in cities as well as rural areas.

Vets began to educate people about animal welfare. This vet worked in a cinema foyer as part of a 1950 campaign with the RSPCA to make the public better aware of their pets' health.

Vets kept written records about each of their patients. They encouraged owners to bring pets in for regular check-ups.

From the 1950s, veterinary medicine developed alongside human medicine. Today, vets use hi-tech x-ray equipment and can perform operations such as heart surgery.

Fraser

The family have two ginger cats. Fraser belongs to Robert and is more than 10 years old.

The other ginger cat is called Lester, and belongs to their mother.

Nicola

"I love living in Blackpool, with the amusements and the piers and the beach."

Nicola is 10 years old and lives in the seaside resort of Blackpool, in the northwest of England. Her family own a sweet factory that makes different types of hard, sugary sweets. Because there are big, boiling pots of sugar, the factory is not a place for children, but Nicola and her brother, David, help out with some small tasks.

Nicola has a collection of kites to fly on the beach. This one only cost 99p but it flies the best!

BLACKPOOL TOWER
The Blackpool Tower, built in 1894, is a landmark of this British holiday destination. Every year tourists come to enjoy Blackpool's amusement arcades, rides, piers, fast-food stalls and beach life.

Cousin Elliot works in the factory.

MAKING ROCK
The factory manufactures sticks of rock, a traditional Blackpool souvenir. Sugar is boiled at 150ºC in big copper pots. Dyes are added, then the mixture is poured onto a cooling table and is pulled and stretched to stop it solidifying.

This is a modern replica of an old-fashioned carousel.

GOLDEN MILE
Nicola's house is five minutes away from the "Golden Mile", where many of Blackpool's major attractions can be found. She also likes going for a carousel ride on the North Pier.

One of Nicola's most treasured toys is this wind-up carousel, which her Nan gave her.

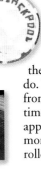

LETTERING
Putting letters in rock is a skilled task, which less than 100 people in the country know how to do. The letters are made from sugar mixture, 50 times bigger than they appear in the rock. Then more sugar mixture is rolled around them.

At the Sea Life Centre, Nicola fed baby sharks with dead eels. She was scared the sharks would bite her.

Grandfather   Grandmother   Father

LIGHTING UP
Nicola's favourite time of year is the autumn, when the whole sea-front shines with electric lights called the Blackpool Illuminations. Autumn is Blackpool's busiest time, when Nicola's family sell most of their rock.

Workers wear hats to keep their hair out of the rock mixture.

BATCH ROLLER
The giant bar of rock is thrown into the batch roller machine, which rolls it until it is long and very thin.

In the holidays, Nicola and David help feed sticks of rock into the wrapping machine.

Cousin   David   Mother
Elliot   Nicola

Swirling and cutting are done by hand.

ROCK TABLES
The long stick of rock comes out of the batch roller, then is twisted, to create the swirling effect. Then it is cut into small sticks.

WRAPPING
A worker can wrap 10 sticks of rock a minute, but the machine can wrap 80 per minute.

THE FACTORY
Nicola's grandfather started his sweet factory, Stanton and Novelty Confectioners, in the 1970s. Nicola's father now runs the business. The factory makes 4.5 tonnes of sweets a week. These are sold around Britain, and exported worldwide.

"This lollipop took three hours to make and is 50 times larger than ordinary lollipops."

LOOKING BACK

1890 FAMILIES HAVE BEEN GOING ON HOLIDAY to Blackpool for over 200 years. At first only wealthy people could afford to get there, but in 1840, a railway link was built so that families from Manchester, Liverpool and other northern towns could get to Blackpool by train. They came to bathe in the sea but soon there were lots of other attractions. Most of Blackpool's landmarks were built in the last 40 years of the 19th century – the North, Central and South Piers, the electric tram and the Blackpool Tower. One treat for children was to go on a donkey ride along the beach.

1896 Children loved to ride on the huge ferris wheel, built in 1896. It had 30 cars, each of which could hold 30 people.

1950s Families visiting Blackpool in the 1940s and 1950s often stayed in Bed and Breakfasts. They would start the day with a traditional breakfast of fried eggs and bacon served by their landlady.

1960s From the 1960s, many families began going on cheap package holidays abroad. But Blackpool remained popular. Teenagers love *The Big One*, which opened in 1994. It is the biggest rollercoaster in the country.

When I grow up, I would like to be an artist. I would help my dad at the factory, but I wouldn't like to be the boss because I see that my dad works too hard. When I'm grown up, I think that sweets will be different, with new ingredients and flavours.

Nicola

Nicola's bucket and spade

Nicola found this stone on the beach. She painted the rabbit's face then gave the stone to her grandma.

SWEETS
Each year the sweet factory makes almost one million lollipops and three-quarters of a million sticks of rock. More than 21 tonnes of sugar are bought every 10 days. Three or four new designs are created at the factory every year. Children buy lollipops with fun new designs, but older people often prefer the more traditional pink rock.

Nicola likes the fruit sweets because they look and taste like real fruit.

TJ

"I like moving around. Instead of two or three friends, I've got lots."

About 20 large lorries are needed to transport the circus tents, equipment, and people around the Southeast.

LONG TRAILER

TJ and his family live in these trailers all year round. From spring until autumn, they travel around the Southeast with the circus. From November until March they return to live in Peterborough, where their relatives live.

TJ's parents shipped their trailer from the United States. American trailers provide many of the amenities of living in a house, such as a washing machine and microwave.

For much of the year, eight-year-old TJ moves to a new place and goes to a different school almost every week. His parents perform in one of Britain's most famous circuses, Zippo's Circus, which moves around Southeast England.

KEEPING TRACK

TJ brings his Educational Record when he goes to a new school. It tells the teachers what he has been taught so far.

BIG TOP

Zippo's Circus is put up on playing fields, sports grounds or commons. It takes as many as 50 people up to four hours to assemble the Big Top. TJ often helps. He likes the exercise he gets from lifting up the heavy poles that support the canvas roof.

The circus ticket office can sell up to 1,000 tickets for afternoon or evening performances. The tickets cost between £3.50 and £12. The audience choose between seats around the ring, or futher away on the grandstand or sides.

TJ's mother guides the horses around the ring and encourages them to do tricks. While his parents perform in the evenings, TJ may stay in his trailer or watch.

SHOWTIME

In the centre of the Big Top is a ring where clowns, jugglers, trapeze artists, acrobats and horse trainers perform. They do amazing feats of courage and daring. This year TJ's father, Tom, balanced with one foot on each of two galloping horses while another five horses rode under his legs.

TRAINING TIME

Circus artists spend the winter months developing their acts, while the circus is not showing. Tom practises every day to develop enough strength to stand on the horse's backs during the show. TJ used to be a tumbler with a group of Moroccan acrobats when he was four, doing backflips and tumbles. He has not practised enough gymnastics recently and could not do these at the moment.

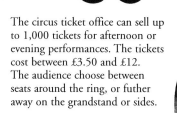

HORSE CARE

TJ's family have nine Palomino horses and a Shetland pony. The horses have their own tent for sleeping in and a paddock for grazing at each site. The high standards of horse care at Zippo's Circus have won praise from animal welfare officers throughout the country.

TJ can do the splits with his left leg forwards.

ACROBATICS
TJ is an only child. His best friends at the circus are two brothers, the acrobats Giuseppe and Manuel. Here, Giuseppe throws Manuel in the air to do a somersault and land back on his hands.

CLOWNING AROUND
Zippo himself is a clown. All the clowns in his circus are great comedians, making everyone laugh during their tumbling feats and musical numbers.

"My favourite acts are acrobats and clowns. Clowns are very, very funny. Acrobatics is fun, when you're upside down doing twists and turns."

Peter Pan is TJ's pet. He is a Shetland pony.

LOOKING BACK

1900 TJ's family have been in the circus almost since it began. Modern circus dates from the mid-18th century when Philip Astley found that it was easy to stand on a horse's back when it galloped around a ring, and invited audiences to watch him. The first Big Tops were put up after 1825. By 1900 circus acts included high wire walks, trapeze stunts, clowns, acrobats and wild animals. Circuses toured the world.

This illustration of the Tower Circus in Blackpool is from their souvenir booklet of 1938.

THE ROBERT BROTHERS FAMILIES

1950s Circus families became famous. Each generation was trained from childhood in the skills and disciplines of one or more acts. But by the 1950s, circus audiences were shrinking. People preferred to watch TV or go to the movies. Circus families began to break up. The Roberts family was one of the few that remained in the circus.

The Roberts family in the 1950s.

Circuses did winter performances in theatres until audiences began to shrink.

1980s Circuses responded to shrinking audiences by creating ever more fantastic acrobatic and clowning acts. They often perform once more to packed houses.

Even though we move around a lot, I always go back to the same schools every year, and I get to see all my old friends. The best bit is when I get to go on school trips. In the future, I think everything will be automatic. You'll just press a button and the whole Big Top will just pop up.

T. J.

Thomas

"I love living in Westminster Abbey."

Nine-year-old Thomas lives in Westminster Abbey, one of the oldest and most important churches in London. His father, Jonathan, is a priest at the Abbey and Thomas's family lives in a small house tucked away within the Abbey's walls. Thomas is an acolyte, or helper, at his local church, St Matthew's.

RELIGIOUS FAITH
Thomas's family have been devout Christians for generations. His grandfather, great-grandfather and great-great-grandfather were all priests. Above is one of Thomas's favourite paintings, a Christian icon.

INCENSE HOLDER
When Thomas's father is not holding any services himself, Thomas and his family attend a service at a nearby church, St Matthew's. Here the priest swings a thurible, or incense holder, to release a sweet scent.

Mother · AnnaMary · Father · Thomas

Persian incense · Greek incense · Incense boat

SECRET GARDEN
Although the Abbey is in the centre of London, it has large lawns behind it where Thomas and his four-year-old sister, AnnaMary, like to play. But tourists sometimes watch them.

BOAT BOY
One of Thomas's jobs at church is to spoon incense from a "boat" onto the hot coals which are inside the thurible.

COVERED WALKWAY
Thomas's house is reached via a number of covered walkways around open air courtyards called cloisters. When they have heavy shopping, Thomas's family use a wheelbarrow to cart it through the cloisters.

The children's favourite place to play is in the small courtyard in front of their house where tourists aren't allowed.

This white clerical collar is called a dog collar.

ON THE MOVE
Jonathan was working in an Oxfordshire parish when Thomas was born. AnnaMary became the first child to be born in Westminster Abbey since 1953 after the family moved there. Jonathan will not serve at the Abbey for much longer. Thomas must go to a new school and make new friends wherever his family moves to.

FAVOURITE BOOKS
Thomas most enjoys reading *The Chronicles of Narnia* by C S Lewis. He sometimes listens to the stories on tape because he finds the books difficult to read easily.

SPELL-CHECKER
Thomas is dyslexic, which means he has difficulty with spelling and reading. He uses a computer to check his spelling.

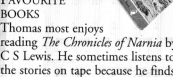

ROCK COLLECTION
Thomas has been collecting rocks and minerals for three years. He likes the minerals because they sparkle.

WESTMINSTER ABBEY
Thomas's family has lived in the Abbey for six years. The Abbey has played an important part in British history for hundreds of years. Since the 11th century, English kings and queens have been crowned there, including our queen. Every day, hundreds of tourists from all over the world visit this historic place of worship.

All the priests at Westminster Abbey wear red cassocks. The only other priests in Britain allowed to wear red cassocks are the Queen's Chaplains, and others who serve the royal family.

The belt that Jonathan is wearing is called a cincture.

Cincture is pronounced sinc-ture

When he is helping at church, Thomas wears a black woollen coat called a cassock.

He puts a long white shirt called a cotta over the cassock.

" The only part I don't like about wearing a cassock is that it feels like there are billions of buttons. Really there are seven."

Underneath the cassock, Thomas wears his ordinary clothes.

Thomas

" My sister and I are the only children who live at the Abbey. It's annoying having so many tourists visiting where you live every day. I haven't decided what to be when I grow up, but I know I don't want to be an astronaut – I wouldn't like to get caught in a black hole and stretched like a strand of pasta. I like it when they make peace agreements for Northern Ireland. I say prayers about how happy I am. "

LOOKING BACK

1890 THOMAS'S GREAT-GREAT-GRANDFATHER, Canon Hicks, was a clergyman at the end of the 19th century. At that time many people were actively Christian. They went to church on Sundays, said their prayers and read their Bibles at home. British missionaries travelled abroad, particularly to India and Africa, and converted millions of people to Christianity.

Thomas's great-grandfather, Canon Hicks

Thomas's great-great-grandfather, Canon Edward Barry Hicks

Adults and children wore their "Sunday best" clothes to church.

1960s During the 20th century, church attendance fell rapidly. When Thomas's grandfather was a vicar in the 1960s, many people, particularly in cities, rejected religious standards and structures. Today, only one in ten people is a church member. But Christians like Thomas's family are more active than ever, working in their churches and the wider community to give help to those in need.

1990s Thomas's great-great-grandfather was the vicar of Holy Cross church in Haltwhistle, Northumberland. This country church is still a centre of village life. More than 40 people attend Sunday services.

1970s Traditionally, many Christian children attended Sunday School to learn about religion. In the 1970s, Sunday School was renamed "Children's Church" or "Young Church".

Ruby

"In England I feel Bangladeshi; in Bangladesh I feel English."

Ten-year-old Ruby lives in the Yorkshire city of Sheffield. Her parents are from Bangladesh, which was part of Pakistan, and India before that. They practise the Hindu religion. As well as learning about Hinduism, Ruby learns Indian classical dance.

Indian classical dance is performed barefoot. Ruby wears ankle bells when she dances, to ring out the rhythm.

RUBY'S STREET
Ruby lives in a mostly Asian neighbourhood, full of families from Pakistan, India and Bangladesh. Ruby's aunt is a social worker, working in the close-knit Asian community. Ruby can walk to school from her house in less than two minutes. Many of her fellow pupils are Asian.

Ruby's family speak Bengali, the main language of Bangladesh, at home, so that the children won't forget how to speak it.

Ruby

Puruby

OUT TO PLAY
Ruby is responsible for looking after her brother, Dhrabo (aged three) and sister, Puruby (aged six) at the weekends. She often takes them to the park.

DANCING
Every Saturday, Ruby attends Indian classical dancing classes in Sheffield. She is sometimes chosen to dance in special performances. Classical Indian dance is over 2,000 years old. The dances tell stories, including ancient Hindu epics such as the *Ramayana*. Each movement of the arms, face and feet describes a particular character, mood or action. Here Ruby acts out the movement of the sea, with her hands playing the motions of the waves.

This beautiful golden necklace and earrings belong to Ruby's mother. Ruby is allowed to wear them when she performs her Indian classical dance.

Ruby likes wearing decorative bindi stickers.

RED-BRICK HOUSE
Ruby has lived in this house all her life. As in many Asian families, her relatives live close by. Her maternal grandmother lives a few doors down, and Ruby sees her every day. Her grandmother loves gardening, and planted all the flowers in Ruby's front garden.

PUTTING ON A SARI
The traditional dress for a Hindu woman is a sari. When Ruby is older, she will wear a sari every day, but now she only wears one when she is performing Indian classical dance. A sari is a piece of cloth, about five metres long, which is tied around the body to make a dress. Inexperienced sari wearers often use a safety-pin to keep the sari in place over their shoulder.

To tie her sari, Ruby first tucks one end into her petticoat.

Ruby pleats the other end, then brings it around the body and places it neatly over her shoulder.

A blouse and petticoat are always worn under a sari.

A sari can be made of cotton, silk or polyester. Sari fabrics come in beautiful colours and are embroidered.

Ruby then pleats the remaining middle part of the sari and tucks it in at the front.

Ruby always wears bangles with her sari.

Puruby means "rainbow" in Bengali. Ruby was named after the precious red stone.

"I am sad when I think of all the terrible floods in Bangladesh. I would like to be a doctor when I grow up, so I can help people."

PRAYING

Like many Hindus, Ruby and her family pray mainly at home. They have a shrine adorned with pictures of the gods they pray to – Krishna, Lakshmi and Saraswathi. Ruby also prays at a shrine in her grandmother's house.

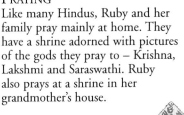

Ruby normally wears long skirts and trainers, but on special occasions she wears her *lenga*, a dress traditionally worn by young Hindu girls. Ruby's *lenga* was bought recently for the *Durga* (dedicated to the Goddess Durga) *Puja*, a Hindu autumn festival which lasts for 10 days.

Ruby prays for her family's health and wealth, and for help if she has to pass a test at school.

Ruby

I've only ever lived in England, but every other year we visit our family in Bangladesh. I like England. Here, we can celebrate Christmas and Easter as well as our Hindu festivals. We eat cornflakes for breakfast but the rest of our meals are always curries.

LOOKING BACK

1983 BY THE TIME RUBY'S PARENTS came to Sheffield from Bangladesh in 1983, there were more than a million Hindus in Britain. Many Asian people had emigrated to Britain from the 1950s onwards. Bangladeshis began arriving in Britain from the 1970s. Most were Muslim, but some were Hindus.

Ruby's family in the 1980s before they came to Britain.

1980s Asian young people were proud to be British and Asian. They began to create a culture of their own. For example, Bhangra, a mixture of Indian music and Western dance music, became popular. One big change was that Asian newlyweds moved out of their parents' homes, as did their non-Asian friends, though they still looked to their parents for advice and support.

A Hindu bride is beautifully made up for her wedding.

1995 Like Ruby, most Hindus still practise their religion. Customs have been adapted to suit life in Britain. For example, children celebrating *Diwali*, a festival of light, make traditional *pakoras* (fried food) and eat sandwiches and sweets. A beautiful new Hindu temple was opened in northwest London in 1995.

Saraswathi is pronounced sar-as-wah-tee

Michael

"I love the sea, but I worry about my dad when the seas are rough."

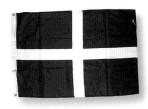

Cornish people have always thought of themselves as a distinct part of Britain. Michael waves his Cornish flag when he supports Cornish rugby teams.

Michael is 10 years old and comes from Cornwall, a county on the western tip of England. His parents are divorced. He and his elder brother, David, spend weekends with their father, Mark, in Port Isaac, but during the week they live with their mother in nearby Fowey. Wherever he is, Michael takes every opportunity to go swimming, surfing or sailing.

PORT ISAAC
Michael's father and grandfather have lived in Port Isaac all their lives. Port Isaac is a seaside village of little more than 700 people, 10 miles from the nearest town. Some villagers are fishermen who catch crabs and lobsters; others work in the tourist industry; many are retired.

A year ago, Michael took up skateboarding. He practises in the lane just outside his father's house. This is his third skateboard.

Lifejacket has built-in buoyancy and a safety harness to attach to the boat in heavy seas.

BEACH BOY
Michael boogie boards in Port Isaac when the waves are big enough. He swims out to where the waves break, paddles towards shore as fast as he can when he sees a big wave coming, then rides the wave kneeling or lying on his board. He and his friends also like diving off the breakwater that protects the harbour from the sea.

MARK'S HOUSE
Before his parents were divorced, Michael lived here all of the time. Now he just lives here at weekends with his father and his father's partner, Candy. Michael and his elder brother David, aged 12, share a bedroom here and at their mother's house.

Helmet has visor to keep spray out of eyes.

The Port Isaac lifeboat station houses a five-metre inflatable boat for use close to shore.

LIFEBOAT CREW
Mark is a volunteer in the Royal National Lifeboat Institution (RNLI). When someone is in danger at sea, the coastguard contacts the Port Isaac lifeboat station manager and sets off the pagers. The station manager fires two rockets, called maroons. When Mark gets paged or hears the maroons, he rushes to the station, puts on his drysuit and helps to launch the lifeboat.

Cornwall is famous for its Cornish pasties, delicious pastry pies filled with meat and vegetables or cheese and onion.

A crew member could die in 15 minutes in freezing water without a drysuit, which has built-in rubber boots.

DAD'S PASTIES
Mark owns a butcher's shop. As well as meat, Mark sells Cornish pasties. When Michael and David stay in Port Isaac, they eat pasties for lunch every day. Michael and David sometimes help their father in the shop – cleaning the meat trays or putting meat in big refrigerators. If Mark's pager goes off or they hear the maroons, Mark has to leave the shop immediately.

HOME SAFELY
In the summer, Mark's crew can be called out daily to rescue swimmers, boats caught in rough seas or people trapped in caves by the tide. While Mark is out, Michael and David wait anxiously for his return. When he gets back, they hose seawater off his drysuit. They put talcum powder inside the suit after he has taken it off, so it is easier to put on again.

"When I'm at my dad's, I go body boarding with my boogie board. I call my friends and if the surf is good, off we go!"

A wet suit keeps Michael warm when he is boogie boarding in the freezing-cold sea.

Michael straps his boogie board to his right wrist to prevent him losing it in the water.

"*When I grow up, I'd like to be a rugby player. If I'm not, I'll probably be in the RNLI. You have to be a strong swimmer, and I am a pretty strong swimmer. I would like to be the helmer, and steer the boat, but after the other day, when my dad's boat got smashed against the rocks, I'm not so sure about joining the RNLI. I suppose I'll be braver when I grow up.*"

Michael

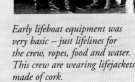

Michael plays wingback or fullback in his local youth rugby team, the Wadebridge Camels.

LOOKING BACK

1800 GOING OUT IN A LIFEBOAT may be dangerous for Mark, but 200 years ago it would have been more so. The first lifeboat, "The Original", was invented by Henry Gatehead at the beginning of the 19th century. It was no more than an open rowing boat. It held about 10 lifeboatmen, who propelled the boat through rough seas by sheer muscle power.

Early lifeboat equipment was very basic – just lifelines for the crew, ropes, food and water. This crew are wearing lifejackets made of cork.

1824 A national charity was eventually set up in 1824 to raise money for lifeboats. In its first year, 12 new lifeboats were built and 342 people were saved from drowning. In 1854, this charity became the Royal National Lifeboat Institution.

Lifeboats were originally launched from horse-drawn carriages, but by 1910, they were mostly steam driven. The first motor-driven lifeboat was used in the Orkneys in 1908.

Today, there are 223 RNLI lifeboat stations in the UK and the Republic of Ireland, with 306 lifeboats.

1970s This is Mark and his RNLI crew-mates more than 20 years ago. Traditionally, crews were fishermen but by the 1970s crew members came from many professions, including shopkeepers like Michael's father. Over the years, children have been particularly active in fundraising for the RNLI. They have organized sponsored events and jumble sales. Over 20,000 belong to the RNLI's young people's club, "Storm Force".

RNLI collecting tin

Stephen

"I taught myself to play the melodica, but daddy teaches me Irish tunes."

Stephen is 10 years old and lives on the border of County Tyrone and County Armagh in Northern Ireland. This area is celebrated as the apple orchard of Ireland. Stephen's family are proud of their Irish culture – they play Irish music and Stephen goes to Irish dancing classes every week.

"We love climbing trees and playing at the bottom of the garden where there are plenty of nettles we can bash down with sticks."

BUNGALOW
Stephen lives with his parents and two brothers, Conall and Ruairi, in the house that his father grew up in. While his grandparents were still living there, Stephen's family lived in a mobile home in the garden.

COUNTRY LIVING
In the autumn, Stephen helps pick apples and gather windfalls in the orchard behind his house. Good apples are packed into boxes for eating but the bruised ones are squashed to make cider.

Apples are ready to pick from the trees from late summer.

IRISH MUSIC
Stephen's father, Peter, makes packaging for a living, but his great love is making traditional Irish music. He plays the fiddle, accordion, tin whistle, flute and *Uileann* (pronounced elen) pipes. He has taught Stephen Irish tunes to play on his melodica.

Accordion

CHAPEL
Stephen's family is Roman Catholic. On Sundays, Stephen serves as an altar boy, helping the priest at his local chapel, St Peter's.

The Melodica is a wind instrument.

Uileann pipes

IRISH DANCING
Stephen's mother teaches Irish dancing, and Stephen has learnt to dance since he was three. Irish *ceilidh* dancing is like Scottish country dancing. In "sets" of two, three or four couples, dancers make a sequence of shapes, such as circles and double lines. Dances include jigs, reels and hornpipes and are accompanied by traditional Irish music. Solo Irish dancing is mainly fast footwork.

The upper body is kept as straight as possible in solo dancing.

A good sense of balance is essential.

This is a basic step – footwork can become much more complicated.

The faster and more varied the footwork, the more exciting the dance.

Dancers wear soft, leather shoes.

UILEANN PIPES
These are similar to Scottish bagpipes. *Uileann* means "elbow" in Irish. The piper pumps the bellows with his elbow and fingers the pipes to sound notes.

Stephen's mother and the prizewinners

The McBride School of Dancing crest

Snowy is the family dog and chases them round the house. Stephen also enjoys pony riding and would love to have a horse.

VICTORY SMILES
Stephen travels with his mother all over Ireland for dancing competitions called *feisanna* (pronounced feshanna) in Irish. Last year, they entered the Ulster Championships at Ballymena. Stephen and the others danced his favourite dance, the Four-hand Reel, and they won a prize.

GAELIC FOOTBALL
Stephen supports Tyrone Gaelic football team. A Gaelic football team has 15 players. They punch, bounce or kick the ball into (three points) or directly over (one point) the rectangular goal-net. Stephen also supports Manchester United.

Conall is Stephen's three-year-old brother.

Ruairi (pronounced Rory) is eight years old.

LOOKING BACK

1900 STEPHEN TAKES PART in an ancient dance tradition. From the 17th century, throughout Northern and Southern Ireland, villagers held dances every week. But many Irish people died in a terrible famine in the 19th century, and the traditional culture was threatened. In the late 19th and early 20th centuries, people all over Ireland took up their ancestors' music and dance again.

1950 Many Irish people emigrated to escape the famine. In the 1950s and 60s, Irish communities all over the world revived Irish dancing to show they still felt attached to their old country.

Michael Flatley

1990s In the 1990s the stage show *Riverdance,* which featured lightning-quick solo Irish dancing, took the world by storm. Huge numbers of children and adults alike now want to learn how to dance like the show's star, Michael Flatley, and classes such as Stephen's mother's are very popular.

Stephen

" *When I grow up, I'd like to be an Irish dancing teacher like my mummy and teach my favourite dance, the Four-hand Reel. Only I'd have to teach the Heavy Jig too, which is very difficult. I wish there would be a better level of peace in Northern Ireland. I think they should ban handguns and that.* "

Cultivated mushrooms are grown on manure.

MUSHROOM SHEDS
Stephen's grandfather used to grow mushrooms in sheds at the bottom of the garden. Stephen's father now uses the sheds to store mushroom trays which he sells to mushroom farmers throughout Ireland.

Field mushrooms are found in the wild in meadows and pastures.

Rhiannon

"My favourite dance is the Highland Fling."

Rhiannon is seven years old and lives in a hotel on the beautiful island of Bute, 60 kilometres west of Glasgow. Rhiannon's father runs the hotel and her mother is a teacher. Rhiannon helps her father before and after school. But often she is too busy horse riding, Highland dancing or visiting the seals that live on Bute's shores.

BUTE FERRY
Bute is 24 kilometres long and 6.5 kilometres wide. Rhiannon, her parents, grandparents, uncles, aunts and cousins all live on Bute. There is no road to the mainland. A car ferry brings food and other supplies to the island. During the winter, it's impossible to leave the island after 5.30 p.m.

THE COMMODORE
Many of Bute's inhabitants work in the tourist industry – in hotels, shops and the transport system. Rhiannon's family own *The Commodore* hotel, which has six rooms for guests. They live in a flat in the hotel.

Sliding down the bannisters is Rhiannon's favourite thing to do in the hotel.

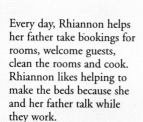

Every day, Rhiannon helps her father take bookings for rooms, welcome guests, clean the rooms and cook. Rhiannon likes helping to make the beds because she and her father talk while they work.

Everywhere that Rhiannon goes, Big Bear goes with her.

TIME TO DANCE
Rhiannon is learning Highland dance, the native dance of the Scottish Highlands. Most dances are solo. They consist of a sequence of precise steps and energetic leaps that require grace and stamina. Dancers are accompanied on the bagpipes.

HARDY HORSES
Rhiannon goes horse riding on strong, little Shetland ponies. These are the smallest ponies in Britain, so it doesn't hurt if she falls off. Shetlands originally came from the Shetland Islands, northeast of Scotland.

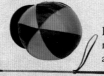
Rhiannon's riding hat and crop

Rhiannon has won many rosettes in riding competitions.

HIGHLAND FLING
Rhiannon's favourite dance is the Highland Fling. This was probably originally based on the movements of a deer. It is danced on the spot and takes about three minutes to complete. Here Rhiannon is practising some of the steps.

Dancers wear tartan kilts. Old Highland families have their own tartan patterns. Rhiannon doesn't come from such a family, so she wears any tartan she likes.

"When I do my Highland dancing, we dance to bagpipe music. Sometimes it's on tape, but sometimes we have live players."

" _I like living in a hotel because you get to meet a lot of people, as there are always people around. The only bad thing is that my dad is always busy. I would like to join the circus when I grow up, and do lots of backflips. If I don't get into the circus, I'd like to be a vet. I would like it if nobody in the world was ever allowed to kill animals._ "

Rhiannon

"This is my wee frilly blouse. The only part of a dancing outfit I don't have is socks. They should be tartan like my kilt."

SEAL WATCHING
Whenever Rhiannon's father isn't too busy, he takes her trout fishing in Loch Fad (right) or to Scalpsie Bay on the west side of Bute. Here she can watch seals huddle together on rocks or wallow in the shallow waters of the beach.

The seals on the north end of Bute are mostly common seals.

Rhiannon dances in soft, leather "ghillie" pumps.

LOOKING BACK

Food did not keep for long. Meals had to be made from fresh ingredients using basic equipment.

Wealthy people and hotel owners employed servants to help them. Servants worked up to 18 hours a day, and although board and lodging came with the job, their pay was very low.

1900 RHIANNON MAY HAVE to help her father, but cooking and cleaning for guests is a lot quicker now than it would have been 100 years ago. Then, everyone washed clothes and sheets by hand, and squeezed them through a mangle to get the water out. Wooden floors were scrubbed and carpets beaten to get the dust out. Fires had to be lit very early on winter mornings to warm rooms.

These laundresses are scrubbing clothes by hand using washboards and brushes.

In the 20th century, a number of labour-saving household inventions speeded up domestic work and reduced the need for servants. These inventions mostly relied on electricity. Most houses were connected to an electric power supply by about 1940.

1913 The first domestic fridges appeared in 1913. By the 1950s, most people owned a fridge. Food could be stored for days and meals could be prepared in advance.

1916 The Hoover company started selling vacuum cleaners in 1916. This is a modern Dyson cleaner.

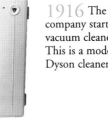

1940s Washing machines allowed housewives and hotel owners to wash a load of bed linen in less than an hour.

Jojo

"I won't be a thatcher because I don't think it's a girl's thing to do."

Jojo is seven years old and lives with her nine-year-old sister, Katy, and their parents in the Cotswold village of Chipping Campden. The houses in her village are made from limestone, which was quarried from the local hills. Jojo's father is a thatcher. He makes roofs of stacked straw, or thatch, which top many Cotswold cottages.

Jojo made this mask out of papier mâché. She calls it a millennium mask as it's a British child in the year 2000.

Katy likes painting with pastels and charcoals and doing crafts. She made these Cotswold sheep.

OLD HOME
Jojo and her family live in the centre of Chipping Campden's main street, opposite the Market Hall. They live in a flat above a shop, which completes a long row of 17th-century Cotswold stone buildings.

Jojo has learnt to say many of the prayers in her book off by heart.

HOLY COMMUNION
The family go to St Catharine's Catholic church. Jojo recently made First Communion, at which she was given a Host (wafer) and wine by the priest. She got a prayer book, rosary and certificate to mark the occasion. Jojo and Katy will make their Confirmation when they are 12 or 13. They will say prayers to show they have chosen their faith of their own free will.

BEDROOMS
The sisters have their own rooms. Katy doesn't always let Jojo into her room during the day. Sometimes, though, Jojo feels lonely at night, and Katy lets her sleep in her bedroom.

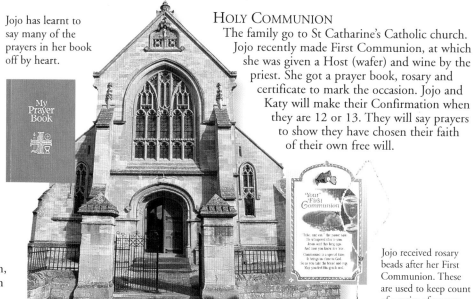

St Catharine's Catholic church

Jojo received rosary beads after her First Communion. These are used to keep count of a series of prayers such as "Hail Mary".

SWAN THEATRE, STRATFORD

Jojo lives near Stratford-Upon-Avon, where the great playwright, William Shakespeare, was born in 1564. Stratford has several theatres. Jojo and Katy saw *The Lion, the Witch and the Wardrobe* (adapted from C S Lewis's books) in Stratford.

AWAY FROM IT ALL
Coach-loads of tourists come into Chipping Campden early every morning. Jojo and Katy play and cycle in the local park when their street gets too busy to play in.

The whole family go in the car to watch the torchlight procession into the village the night before the Wake.

Jojo loves the morris dancers, who perform English folk dances, dressed in white clothes and bells.

SCUTTLEBROOK WAKE
On the weekend after spring bank holiday, the village holds a sports day, called the Cotswold Olympics, followed by the Scuttlebrook Wake, or fair. The sisters visit the many stalls and watch the street entertainment. Jojo wants to join in the Maypole dancing when she's older.

"After the millennium, I hope that teachers will give us less homework because we've got so many hobbies that we don't have time to do them. When I grow up, I don't know what I'd like to be. But I'm sure by that time, there will be new and different jobs, and if there is one I may enjoy, I will do that."

Jojo

LOOKING BACK

1800s UNTIL THE 17TH CENTURY, most houses had timber frames and thatched roofs. Thatchers, like Jojo's father, were constantly busy hammering down wooden pegs to secure the thatch and shaping it neatly into place. But wood and thatch were very prone to fire. By the 1800s, houses were usually built from brick and stone, with tiled roofs. Today, those thatched cottages that remain are very popular, and thatchers such as Jojo's father are much in demand.

Katy has brought her school class to watch her father work and learn about thatching. Jojo will soon bring her class.

1850s Many beautiful stone buildings were built in the mid-19th century. They have high ceilings and sash windows. Rhiannon's hotel (p44) was built at this time.

1880s Ruby (p38) lives in a red-brick terrace typical of those built in the 19th century for factory workers. The houses had tiny yards and outside toilets. Gardens and indoor bathrooms were added in the 1950s.

1920s In the 1920s, many families moved into new semi-detached or detached suburban homes with large gardens. Fathers commuted into town centres to work. Helene's house (p24) was built in 1928.

1960s After World War I ended in 1918, local councils began to replace city slums with new housing available at low rents. The housing was often arranged in large estates, like Can and Cem's (p62). In the 1960s, many councils built high-rise blocks, which sometimes had too few open spaces and leisure facilities. Today, much work is done to improve high-rise estates.

1970s By the 1970s, millions of adults owned cars. New houses, such as Phillip's (p28) included a garage. Architects experimented with space. Phillip's house doesn't have separate rooms downstairs. It is "open-plan".

Michelle

"I have South African, Cypriot, Russian, Polish, Italian and Lithuanian blood in me."

Thirteen-year-old Michelle has many nationalities in her family. She lives with her parents in East London. Her best friend is her big sister, Olga. They used to play with toys together. Now they give each other makeovers.

" Lots of my family have been killed in wars. Instead of fighting, enemies could have a chess match or some sort of game against each other and whoever wins, wins the argument. "

Michelle

Amy

"The best thing was when my brother and sister were born. The worst was when my dog, Mindy, died."

Twelve-year-old Amy has two sisters and a brother, who she argues with a lot. Her father is a plumber. She often goes with him to people's houses to help him carry and measure things.

" When I grow up, I want to be a hairdresser or a makeup artist because I love to do people's hair. "

Amy

Ollie

"I've fished with my dad since I was a little boy."

Ollie is 11 years old and is the son of a fisherman in Hastings, on the south coast. Hastings has been a fishing port for centuries, and Ollie's family feature in one of the earliest lists of fishermen, dating from 1870. Ollie helps his father, Peter, prepare for fishing trips, filling water bottles and doing other chores.

HASTINGS

Hastings is an historic town. The Battle of Hastings took place nearby in 1066, when Frenchman William the Conqueror invaded England and defeated the English king, Harold. Part of the town is a seaside resort. Elsewhere are the old, cobbled streets of the fishermen's quarter.

BEACH BOATS

Peter keeps his fishing boat in Hastings' harbour. The shore is lined with broad wooden boats, made from oak and elm. They are usually not more than nine metres long by four metres wide. This means that they are light enough to be pushed along the shore and launched by the fishermen.

Ollie makes sure that the trawl nets are free of debris before his father sets out to sea.

Ollie checks that Peter has enough flags to mark the position of trammel nets in the sea.

GRAVELLING

After there has been a storm, Ollie loves to go gravelling – looking for any treasures that may have been washed up on the shore. This chamber pot came up in a trawl after the big storm in 1987. It dates from the 1920s.

Ollie's grandad found this ring when gravelling and gave it to Ollie's Nanny Wend.

Trammelling on the open sea

FISHING NETS

Peter fishes using trawl nets and sometimes trammel nets. A trawl net is dragged through the sea from the back of the boat, trapping fish as it goes. Groups of trammel nets are laid in fleets along the seabed, held down by anchors, and marked by flags; they trap the fish that swim through them. The fisherman returns and gathers in the nets full of fish.

THE CATCH

Depending on the season, Ollie's father and his fellow fishermen catch plaice, cod, sole and dabs. Dabs are considered leftovers and are often given to the "boy ashore". The prime catch is sole, which fetches the best price at market. Sometimes the nets are filled with spider crabs, and Ollie helps to pick them out, as their pincers often get tangled in the nets.

Spider crab

Market where fish is auctioned

The sturgeon's little black eggs are salted to make caviar.

STURGEON

Once Peter caught a sturgeon, whose eggs are the expensive delicacy known as "caviar". There is an ancient British custom that anyone catching a sturgeon must first offer it to the king or queen. Peter offered it to our queen, but she said she didn't have a banquet coming up, so he could keep it.

Ollie's football

BOY ASHORE

The fish are sorted, counted, gutted and packed on the boat. Back on shore, they are taken to the market by the "boy ashore". Ollie's grandfather is a boy ashore; he helps push the boats out to sea and takes the fish to market. At the market the fish are auctioned and sold.

Haddock is often eaten smoked. Some of Ollie's relatives smoke their own fish by hand.

Plaice – a flat white fish

Dover sole – best of the catch

FOOTBALL

Ollie plays football every day in the streets by his house. He also plays every Sunday in a team called Tackleway, in the midfield position. Ollie supports the Arsenal, as his mother originally came from Highbury in London. Once he went and trained in Highbury Stadium.

"In the summer when it's hot, we jump off the harbour wall into the sea. There are about 50 of us. We all jump in, swim along, climb up the wall, and start again."

Ollie

"When I grow up, I'd like to be an engineer, but if not, I'll probably be a fisherman. I know all about fishing as I've been learning since I was a little boy. My dad and grandad have both fished since they were my age. The bit I like about fishing is trawling, but not heaving up the trawl when it's full of fish, because it's too heavy! I also like helping to gut the fish after a catch. I wish in the future there would be more fish, as if I became a fisherman, there won't be many fish left. If the seas weren't polluted, there would be more fish."

LOOKING BACK

1939 WHILE OLLIE'S GRANDFATHER was growing up in Hastings, Britain went to war against Germany and its allies in World War II. By 1940, the Germans had invaded France. German troops were only a short distance away, across the English Channel. It was a terrifying time. Towns along the south coast were on constant alert in case Germany invaded. They were an easy target for German air-raids – there were 85 raids on Hastings alone.

1940 When an air-raid warning siren sounded, everyone rushed to take cover. Many families had shelters in their back garden and would spend the night there, sleeping on narrow bunk beds. Sometimes school was held underground in case of a raid.

Beaches were defended with barbed wire and mines to prevent an invasion. Road blocks were set up and visitors were banned from coastal towns.

Gas attack exercises were carried out in which people practised wearing their masks.

The government thought that the Germans might drop bombs containing poisonous gas, so everyone was given a gas mask, which they had to carry round with them. Ollie's family still have his great-grandmother's gas mask.

1945 One danger on the coast was sea mines. These were planted in the Channel to blow up enemy ships and submarines, but sometimes one washed ashore. This photo, taken in the last year of the war, shows a bomb disposal officer pulling a mine from the sea before disarming it.

Samantha

"I wish that more things were written in Braille."

Eleven-year-old Samantha lives with her mother and father in Maidstone, Kent. Samantha is visually impaired. From birth, she has only been able to distinguish between light and dark. She loves music, and not only sings and writes her own songs, but also plays the drums and marches in the Girls' Brigade.

Samantha loves playing, running around and jumping in the park even though she sometimes falls.

Microphone echoes Samantha's voice

SAMANTHA'S HOUSE
When Samantha leaves her house, she has to use a special cane to feel what is in front of her. At home, Samantha knows every part of her house so well that she never needs to use her cane.

CUDDLING UP
Samantha's room is so full that there is almost no space for a bed. Samantha has a television, a drum kit, a personal stereo and many toys like Sticklebricks. She called her bear "Cuddles" because she likes hugging her.

MUSIC
Toys which have sound effects are Samantha's favourites. She loves listening to music, especially the Spice Girls. "Sporty Spice", Mel C, is her favourite member of the band.

Samantha's "Zube Tube" makes low, vibrating noises when spoken into.

DORTON HOUSE
Samantha attends Dorton House School in Kent. It is run by the Royal London Society for the Blind, which provides education, training and jobs for children and adults who are blind or partially sighted. The 115 pupils at Dorton House have advanced "talking" computers as well as talking calculators and scales. They also have Braille machines, and tactile diagrams and maps.

Boarders live in this part of the school.

GREAT DAY OUT
Samantha is an only child but she is never lonely because she has many friends. Her best friend is called Louise. Once, during the school holidays, Samantha's parents took Louise and Samantha to a theme park.

BRAILLING
Samantha reads and writes in Braille – groups of raised dots making words, which Samantha feels with her fingertips. Writing in Braille is called brailling, and is done on a Braille machine that is like a typewriter. Samantha's grandfather bought her a Braille machine.

Samantha's favourite Talking Book

SCHOOL FRIENDS
During break at school, Samantha and her friends play football in the playground. There are a few more teachers supervising playtime than in sighted schools, to assist any child that needs extra care.

This is Samantha's science book. Her teacher makes pictures and diagrams with raised lines, so Samantha can feel what she has done. The labels to the flower's parts are typed in Braille.

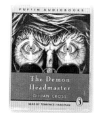

This "talking" calculator announces which number or symbol Samantha presses and the answer to sums.

"I like listening to funny tapes because sometimes in my mind I feel some funny noise or funny word and I can't stop laughing."

LOOKING BACK

1900 A CENTURY AGO, a growing number of people were working to improve the lives of visually impaired people. In the 1820s, Frenchman Louis Braille had developed a system of raised dots, which could be used in various combinations to make the alphabet. In 1838, the London Society for Teaching the Blind to Read (which became the Royal London Society for the Blind) was founded. In 1868, the Royal National Institute for the Blind (RNIB) was set up in Britain to produce literature in Braille.

1918 The RNIB opened up Sunshine Homes for visually impaired children, offering many facilities and opportunities previously only available to sighted children. These homes were in the countryside so children could spend lots of time outside.

1920s Radio broadcasting from the 1920s particularly helped visually impaired people feel more connected to the outside world. Gramophones were another useful invention. The RNIB started up a Talking Books Library in the 1930s. People could borrow a gramophone and recordings of books to listen to.

1930 In the 1930s, the Guide Dogs Association for the Blind began to train dogs to help visually impaired people get around outside. The dogs went to live with visually impaired owners so they could guide them every day, particularly to work. Today, there are well over 400 guide dogs, usually Labradors.

> *When I grow up, I'd like to be a teacher. I'd teach something like PE, because I love jumping around. People annoy me when they barge in front of me. Are they blind? Can't they see the cane? They should take more care. I wish that when I went out shopping more things were written in Braille, so I could read them.*

Samantha likes football and watched every England match in the 1998 World Cup.

DRUMMING
Samantha has been learning to play the drums since she was eight years old. She has a drum kit at home that she practises on, but at school she plays a large drum kit and accompanies a guitarist. She enjoys the drums because she can make as much noise as she likes.

GIRLS' BRIGADE
Samantha is wearing her Girls' Brigade uniform. She has been a Brigade member for six years. The Brigade is like Guides – members earn badges by learning different skills.

"I don't like stairs because you can fall down them. Lifts are safe. You just go in, shut the door and go up and down."

"On the radio they just read things out. On TV they are actually doing things. You can hear 'whoosh' and all the other sound effects."

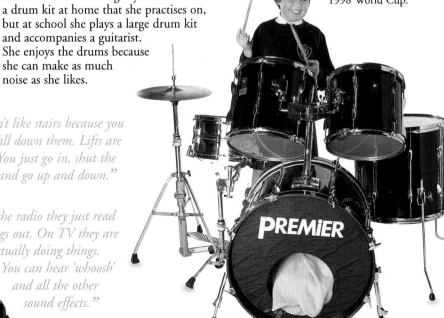

PREMIER

Rudi and Karl share a room with bunkbeds. Rudi usually sleeps on the bottom bunk.

Rudi

"I'd like a big, big house for all my family to live in."

Rudi is seven years old and comes from Belfast, which is the capital city of Northern Ireland. Rudi and his four-year-old brother, Karl, live with their mother, because their parents are divorced. The boys pack an overnight bag and go and stay with their father every other weekend.

BELFAST
The River Lagan flows through Rudi's city, which is home to more than 300,000 people. It was the centre of Northern Ireland's industry last century, earning it the nickname, the "Big Smoke". Since the Good Friday Agreement (see below) the city is flourishing – hundreds of new businesses, shops and restaurants are opening up.

MOTHER'S HOUSE
Rudi's family and both sets of grandparents live doors away from each other on a housing estate. During the summer, the family spend every other weekend in their caravan in the holiday town of Groomsport, near Bangor on the Irish Sea.

Rudi stayed with his Granda and Granny (his mother's parents) on Christmas Eve, while his mother was out buying presents.

BROTHERLY LOVE
After Karl was born, Rudi helped his mother feed him and sometimes bath him. Now Karl and Rudi play together all the time. Rudi's mother has told him to be careful with their toys, as she may not be able to replace them if they lose or break them.

Alien

Millennium Falcon

Oscar is a ginger tom cat who belongs to Rudi's mother. Rudi thinks that Oscar is the coolest cat on the estate. He can always be found roaming the alleyways and often catches mice and brings them home.

LOOKING BACK

1900 DURING THE 19TH CENTURY, Rudi's city grew faster than any other city in the British Isles. Its shipbuilding, linen and tobacco industries boomed. Many smart buildings went up in the city centre. In 1921, Ireland was divided into two. Six provinces in the north, including Belfast, remained in the United Kingdom. The south became the independent Irish Free State in 1922. In the 1930s and 40s, Belfast's industries began to decline. The city was badly bombed in the war. It seemed to the large number of Catholic people that better jobs and housing went to Protestants.

The religious communities in Belfast had been divided since the 19th century. By 1900, Catholic and Protestant children went to different schools. They played separately, even when they lived a few streets apart.

1969 In the 1960s, violence broke out between Protestants and Catholics in Belfast. British troops were sent to keep order and remained there. For 30 years, clashes continued between Catholics and Protestants in a time known as The Troubles.

1998 In 1998, Protestant and Catholic leaders signed the Good Friday Agreement. It was a time of great hope in Belfast that the new generation of Northern Irish children, like Rudi, would have a chance to live in peace in a united community.

"On Sunday mornings, when my mummy is tired, she sleeps and I give my brother breakfast. I let him choose which cereal he wants and let him use a big person's bowl."

When Rudi stays at his father's house, he brings Mo the teddy.

FATHER'S HOUSE
Rudi's father lives half an hour away. Rudi and Karl stay the night when they visit. They take pyjamas, clothes and shoes for the next day in overnight bags. Both boys attend a Protestant Sunday School every Sunday afternoon.

"My best friend is my wee brother, Karl. He makes me laugh all the time. We sleep on bunkbeds and sometimes he plays tricks and kicks me out of bed."

The best part of staying at their father's is using his computer. Rudi designed this picture on it.

PIANO PLAYER
Rudi has been learning to play the piano since he was four years old. He plays a real piano once a week at his lesson. He practises on an electronic keyboard every day at home, which he prefers because it plays tunes on its own.

STORMONT
Rudi's father taught him and Karl how to ride a bike. Rudi has a new bike, and Karl has Rudi's old one. They cycle all over their estate and on the green at the back of their house, which overlooks the Stormont parliament buildings.

"When I grow up, I would like to be a doctor. Most of all, I want to make my granny's arthritis better. If I could have anything, I would like lots of money and to have good health. I wish that bombs wouldn't go off and that people didn't get shot and killed."

Rudi

Judy the dog is seven years old.

FARMHOUSE
Lisa lives with her parents and her brother, Owen. Their remote stone farmhouse is situated on a long, winding road, which cuts through the Arenig mountain range.

Electric generator

If Lisa needs to get up in the night, she has to use a torch.

GENERATOR
Lisa's house does not have mains electricity. The family have an electric generator that runs on diesel fuel. They only use the generator in the evenings. They have a small fridge that runs on gas but keep most of their food in a freezer at a nearby relative's home.

Only five minutes' walk across the fields from Lisa's house is a waterfall that she often visits with Owen. In summer, she paddles in the waterfall and floats on her airbed. In winter, Lisa goes sledging on a nearby hill.

Amy lives in a small field beside Lisa's house.

PET SHEEP
Lisa's favourite time of year is "lambing", when the sheep have their babies in the spring. Lisa goes out onto the mountain to make sure the mothers are well. Above is Lisa's pet sheep, Amy. When Amy was born, her mother died. Lisa bottle-fed Amy and now keeps her as a pet.

After dark, Lisa often sees foxes along the road.

Lisa

"My nearest neighbour lives two miles away."

Ten-year-old Lisa lives with her family in the heart of the Arenig Mountains in North Wales. Lisa's father is a sheep farmer. He has 2,000 sheep which graze on a mountain top. Lisa helps with the sheep, but mostly she likes to wander off on long walks across the mountains with one of the family.

Owen, age 13

SHEEP ON THE HILLS
The sheep graze on the slopes of Moel Llysnant mountain, 800 metres high and two miles from Lisa's house. Lisa's grandfather inherited this grazing land from his father.

"If we don't turn the generator off at night it makes a noise like a drum. I don't like that! I ride my bicycle along the road, because the fields are quite bumpy."

Sometimes Lisa sees badgers on her walks. Once she saw a dead badger on the road that had been run over.

There are very few days on which Lisa doesn't see a wild rabbit!

TO MARKET
Every summer, Lisa helps her father gather the sheep for shearing and dipping (washing them in fluid that stops insects irritating their wool). Owen helps his father sell male lambs at market. They sell female sheep, or ewes, when they are four years old.

Moel Llysnant is pronounced moyle hl-ees-nant

The Welsh translation of *The Runaway Pony*.

Lisa found this jay's feather.

Jays belong to the same bird family as crows and ravens, which Lisa also sees around her home.

Jay

Magpie

Spotting one magpie is supposed to bring bad luck; spotting two brings joy.

Buzzard

A buzzard's mewing call sounds like a baby crying.

WELSH SPEAKING

Lisa wrote out this Welsh poem *Dim Dwr*, "No Water". Her family speaks Welsh at home. Apart from English lessons, all of Lisa's classes at school are taught in Welsh. Lisa loves horse books. She likes reading English, so she borrows books in English from school to read in her spare time. School is five miles from home – a neighbour drives her there.

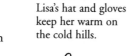

Lisa's hat and gloves keep her warm on the cold hills.

Lisa eats Welsh cakes with butter.

WILDLIFE

Lisa's home is surrounded by rocky hills covered in moss, with no other buildings nearby. The entire area is a haven for wildlife, and when Lisa goes walking, she almost always spots several birds and maybe a wild animal.

Lisa

"*I am Welsh. I speak Welsh at home and with my friends. The only time I ever speak English is during English lessons at school. When I grow up, I'll be a sheep farmer, just like my dad and mum are. But it's not very good for farmers like my dad that the price of sheep has gone down. The only thing I wish would be better in the future is that the price of sheep will go up.*"

HOME LIFE

When the weather is too bad for Lisa to be outside, she often visits a relative. Lisa's mother has seven brothers and four sisters, most of whom live locally. Another thing to do inside is cooking. Lisa made these Welsh cakes, which taste like scones.

LOOKING BACK

1939 WHEN LISA'S GRANDPARENTS were growing up during World War II, country areas of Wales had some extra guests. Big cities such as London, Birmingham and Liverpool were dangerous places to live. Many people were killed and homes destroyed in German bombing raids. From 1939 onwards, thousands of children from cities were "evacuated" – sent away from their families to stay in the country out of danger. Many were sent to Wales, because it was so far from the cities that were being bombed.

Evacuees left cities by train. They travelled in groups with others from their school, accompanied by a teacher. These children were from a Catholic school in South London.

The first evacuees to come to Wales were these children from Birmingham, who arrived at Pontypool station on 2 September 1939. They were matched up with suitable local families and went to live with them.

1940s About 30 evacuees from Birkenhead came to Lisa's local area with two teachers. The young ones went to the village school. The older ones helped out on the farms – feeding animals, milking, collecting firewood, digging and harvesting.

Dim Dwr is pronounced dim dore

Kerry Ann

Kerry Ann's mother puts up posters in towns and villages two weeks before the fair arrives there.

"I've been on the Waltzer hundreds of times, and I've never been sick."

In the summer, ten-year-old Kerry Ann and her fairground family travel all around Oxfordshire. They own three rides, which they set up at fairs. When they are on the road, Kerry Ann doesn't go to school – she does schoolwork in her trailer.

WALTZING AROUND
Kerry Ann's parents own a Waltzer. For four minutes, the track goes round and each of the carriages spins. Kerry Ann has ridden the Waltzer hundreds of times, and can walk between the carriages until it goes at top speed.

Kerry Ann's trailer.

Kerry Ann keeps the fares in her money belt – each ride costs 60p.

The family have a generator to provide electricity during the day, but at night the lights run off the fair's generator.

FAMILY TRAILER
Fairground families don't travel with a particular fair – different families get together in different places. Kerry Ann's family move virtually every week in the summer. They live in two trailers. Kerry Ann sleeps on her own in the smaller trailer. She isn't afraid at night because she locks the door.

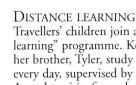

DISTANCE LEARNING
Travellers' children join a "distance learning" programme. Kerry Ann and her brother, Tyler, study a workbook every day, supervised by their mother. A teacher visits for an hour or two each week. In winter, the family park in Eynsham village and the children go to the local school.

The Twister belongs to Kerry Ann's parents. This ride glides in all directions at high speeds and people get squashed against their seats.

JUVENILE RIDE
Kerry Ann looks after the Ladybird ride. It is called a "juvenile" because it's for children, who must be three years old to ride on it alone. Kerry Ann collects the fares then presses the buttons to set off the ride. She gets a percentage of the takings which is put away by her parents for her future.

LOOKING BACK

1860 KERRY ANN'S FAMILY has worked in fairgrounds for almost 150 years. Her great-great-grandfather was a market gardener who fell in love with the fair and opened a coconut shy, where people knocked coconuts out of cups with balls to win prizes. At that time, rides were steam-driven machines such as flying boats and merry-go-rounds.

1920s Going to the fair was a favourite pastime for families on Easter, Whitsun and August bank holidays. People often dressed in their best – and always wore hats.

Kerry Ann's great-grandfather in front of his swinging boats ride in the 1950s.

Kerry Ann's great-aunt Annie and her kiosk.

Bag of candyfloss

1960 Kerry Ann's great-aunt Annie has run a candyfloss kiosk for 40 years. In this time, she has seen less and less people going to fairs. Teenagers have found other ways to spend a night out. The computer-controlled electronic rides bought by Kerry Ann's father since the 1980s are thrilling, but can't compete with the roller coasters at theme parks. Annie worries that by the time Tyler grows up, there won't be any fairs left.

Kerry Ann loves her puppet but doesn't think she's a very good puppeteer or ventriloquist.

"*Each night we go on the fairground rides for free because we are fairground children. We have to be back in our trailers by 10 pm or 10.30 pm if we are lucky.*"

"*It's hard work setting the fair up. When you meet people, you can't get too close, because they may move next week and you will get upset. I think in the future you'll be able to press a button and the fair would fold out and then press it again and the fair would collapse. I wish that there weren't so many robbings, killings and wars in the world. I would ban all guns and knives.*"

Kerry-ann

Tyler, Kerry Ann's six-year-old brother

KIOSK

When Kerry Ann grows up, she would like to own a fairground food kiosk. She thinks this is less hard than working the rides, and you can eat the food when no one is looking. She will have to take a food hygiene and safety certificate when she is about 16 so that she can sell hot food such as hotdogs and burgers. Her great-aunt Annie has already taught her how to make candyfloss.

Jade's family own a helter-skelter and a "juvenile".

Kerry Ann

Tyler

Jade

Jade's brother

FRIENDS

Kerry Ann's best friend is Jade, who she sees at a couple of fairs every year. In between, they speak to each other on their parents' mobile phones. When they are together, in the evenings they go on rides or sit in Kerry Ann's trailer, playing games and telling jokes. Because they go to bed late, they get up late. When their teachers visit, they only come at 9.30 or 10 a.m. in the morning.

Jason

"*Sometimes I get on with my brother; but other times are a completely different matter.*"

Eleven-year-old Jason lives with his mother, his mother's fiancé and his brother, Toby. Because Toby is 16, he doesn't play with Jason much. But they speak French to each other, which Toby learns in school. Their mother is a busy engineer, and Jason washes dishes and sweeps up to help at home.

"*My wishes for the new millennium are that my grandparents live to see me turn into a teenager. I also hope they discover a way of controlling my aunty's disease, rheumatoid arthritis. I also wish that I could have more wishes!*"

Jason

Arliyah

"We usually eat curries and naan but my favourite food is chicken and chips."

Arliyah likes reading adventures and poetry books and playing board games with her brothers. Arliyah's family is Muslim. Her parents are from Pakistan. They speak Urdu and Punjabi at home.

I want the world to be a place where people of all races live in harmony and peace. I hope there will be no more fighting, especially for the people of Iraq, Kashmir, Israel and Northern Ireland.

Arliyah

PURSER HOUSE
Can and Cem live on the fourth floor of their block of flats. They used to have a ground-floor flat, which they preferred because it had a garden. Every other year, the boys go to stay with relatives in Istanbul, the capital of Turkey. Their aunt's house is by the sea, and the boys swim there every day.

Can and Cem

"I'm only five minutes older than Cem."

Can and Cem (pronounced jan and jem) are nine-year-old twins. Their parents are Turkish and came to live in Britain before their eldest son, twelve-year-old Deniz, and the twins were born. The family now live on the Tulse Hill Estate, in Brixton, London.

The family's budgerigar is called Balic, after a Turkish footballer.

FREE TIME
The brothers spend a lot of time outdoors on the estate. They like climbing the trees in a small garden. At home, they have broken most of their toys, so now they buy toys from a shop where everything is £1. They bought a table football game there, which they play with their neighbour, Dean.

Dean, Deniz, Cem, Can

The boys bought these skates in a car boot sale for only £1. Cem taught Can how to skate, and now Can skates better than he does.

Traditional Turkish teapots sit on top of one another. The top pot has the tea leaves, the bottom one has hot water for topping up.

Stuffed vegetables and stuffed vine leaves are called *dolma*.

Tea is drunk black from a glass.

FAMILY AT PRAYER
Can and Cem's family are Muslim – they follow the Islamic religion. Their father prays to Allah (the Muslim name for God) every day at home. Muslims must find a clean place to pray and use a prayer mat, placed in the direction of Mecca in Saudi Arabia, the holy city of Islam. On Fridays, Can and Cem's father prays at the mosque. The twins go with him for Muslim festivals.

The family go to the New Peckham Mosque, which is a converted church.

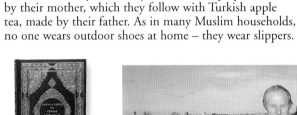

BIG MEAL
The twin's father is a taxi driver; their mother works from home mending clothes. Despite their busy schedules, family mealtimes are important to them. The family eat mostly Turkish food prepared by their mother, which they follow with Turkish apple tea, made by their father. As in many Muslim households, no one wears outdoor shoes at home – they wear slippers.

The twins' father reads them passages from the holy book of Islam, the Qur'an. This was originally in Arabic, but the family have a Turkish translation.

VIEWPOINT
Can and Cem's parents love the superb view over southeast London that they have from their balcony.

"We play with Deniz sometimes; most of the time, we play together."

"We'd like to live in Istanbul, but our brother Deniz would like to live in Wales."

Can

Cem

LOOKING BACK

1900 ISLAM IS THE MAJOR religion throughout large parts of Asia and Africa. There have been Muslims in Britain since the early 19th century, when Muslim sailors and traders from the Middle East settled around major ports. The first mosques had been established in Liverpool and Woking by 1900. Many Muslims from India and Pakistan came to find work in Britain after World War II.

The Qur'an, in Arabic

Prayer mat

In Muslim belief, the last Prophet of Islam was Muhammad, who received a series of revelations from Allah which form the Qur'an. A Muslim has five essential duties. One of these is salat, to pray five times a day. Muslims must also make a pilgrimage to Mecca, Muhammad's birthplace, once in their lifetime.

1990s There are now about 1,500,000 Muslims in Britain. Though bound together by religion, they come from very diverse cultures. Muslims have recently emigrated to Britain from countries as far apart as Iran, Malaysia and Turkey, where Can and Cem's family are from. In the last few years, Muslim refugees have fled to Britain from Somalia in Africa, and Bosnia and Serbia in the former Yugoslavia.

"When I'm older, I'd like to go to the mosque more, like my dad does. I'd like to be a policeman and arrest all the robbers."

Can.

Both Can and Cem like drawing.

The twins speak Turkish with their parents – their mother speaks no English. They cannot read Turkish, so their mother reads poetry to them from this poetry book, which they bought in Istanbul.

IDENTICAL TWINS
Can and Cem don't mind if people get them mixed up. In fact, sometimes each twin pretends to be the other one just to confuse people!

Cem

"We don't have many toys because we've broken them all, but we like to play games like creeping around the house at night when it's dark. I'd like to be a soldier or a commando when I grow up, because I'm strong."

Our travels

"As a family, we were welcomed into the homes of families all over the country."

In one year, Barnabas and I and our baby, Maximilian, travelled to 25 parts of Britain to meet the children we selected for our book. We drove 5,000 miles in our car packed with the lights, cameras and backgrounds for our studio, and Max.

Kerry Ann's younger brother, Tyler, stands behind Max and I on our ride.

While visiting Kerry Ann, who travels with the fair, I took Maximilian on his first fairground ride, the Ladybird. He was only six months old, and fell asleep straight afterwards.

Using a remote control button, Barnabas showed Samantha how to take a picture of herself.

Kieran's big sister showed Maximilian how to pick cherry tomatoes in her family's Guernsey vinery. Ever since, Max's favourite food has been cherry tomatoes.

Michael from Cornwall kept an eye on Max, as he was always trying to pull the tripods and lights down.

"Though we've travelled all over the world, we were fascinated to travel around our own country and discover the different types of people who live here."

"I needed a large space to set up my studio. Sometimes we had a big school hall, but often I had to squeeze the studio into the family's kitchen, and once I crammed the studio into the back of a trailer."

Sometimes, it was impossible to photograph the children's favourite pets. They would only sit still for a second. Trying to photograph two pets and three children was double the trouble.

"We met children and their families who were just like us, and families whose lives were quite different. Seeing how individual we all are made us feel how important it is to celebrate our differences and our similarities."

When Barnabas and I started making the book, Maximilian was a tiny baby. By the end, he was running around all over the place.

Index

Acknowledgments

Barnabas, Anabel and Max would like to say a big thank you to all the parents, brothers and sisters of the children featured in this book.

THEY WOULD ALSO LIKE TO THANK: Peter Loach and the children of Leytonstone School; Christina McGill and Scope; Mary Kingsley and Joy Wilkinson and the Royal London Society for the Blind; Shelley Woodroffe and the Royal National Lifeboat Institution (RNLI); the Commission for Racial Equality; Louise Harwood, Cathy Turner and Lucy Beckett at The Advisory Service for the Education of Travellers; the Scout Association; Co-operation North South; Martin Burton and Zippo's Circus; Marjory Rowan and

The Scottish Official Board of Highland Dancing; The British Tae Kwon-do Council; Anne McIlroy; Latitia Yhap; Safuran Ara; Fay Wertheimer; Anne Johnstone at the *Glasgow Herald*; Rosie Taylor at the *Exeter Express and Echo*; Elizabeth Gomm at the *Blackpool Gazette*; Katrina Bray at the *Guernsey Evening Press*; The Zone Youth Club; Redhills Combined School, Exeter; St Mary's Community Centre, Sheffield; St Catharine's Primary School, Chipping Campden; Alton Riding Stables and the RDA; Lynn Bresler; Rachael Foster; Suzie Gibbs; Natalie Gubbay; Adrienne Hutchinson; Mary Ling; Kate Oliver; Sue Malyan.

Additional photography by: Jane Burton, Andy Crawford, Geoff Dann, Philip Dowell, Mike Dunning, Ellen Hosden, Stephen Oliver.

t = top, b = bottom, l = left, r = right, a = above, c = centre

Blackpool Pleasure Beach Ltd: 33clb; Bridgeman Art Library: 16b, 63c; Collections: 46bl, bc, br; Colorific: 39bca; Colorsport: 11crb; Julian Cotton Photo Library: 54tr; Dorling Kindersley Picture Library/Glasgow Museums: 63tr; Mary Evans Picture Library: 13tcb, 28cr, cra, bc, 35tr, 37cr; John Frost Newspaper Archive: 54cra; Hulton Getty: 11tc, ca, 13tr, 16bra, 19b, 31br, 33cra, 41cr, 43tc, 45bc, bra, 51cla, cr, br, 53trb, 54cr, cl, 57b, clb, 58bl, bca; National Trust Photogaphic Library/Andreas von Einsiedel: 45cl; Popperfoto: 11cla, crb, 15c, 21cr, crb, 25cr, 28br, 39br, 43cra, 51clb, 54b, 57cr; The Riverdance/Anthony Crickmay: 43c; RNIB: 53tr; Royal National Lifeboat Institution: 41bc, cra; Royal Shakespeare Theatre, Stratford: 46bla; Science & Society Picture Library: 33tlb; The Scouts Association: 28clb; Tony Stone Images: 55bra, 63tr; Telegraph Colour Library: 13cl; Topham Picturepoint: 11bc, 15tr, 16bc, 19bra, 21br, 23br, 28c, 31crb, cra, 33tr, 37bra.

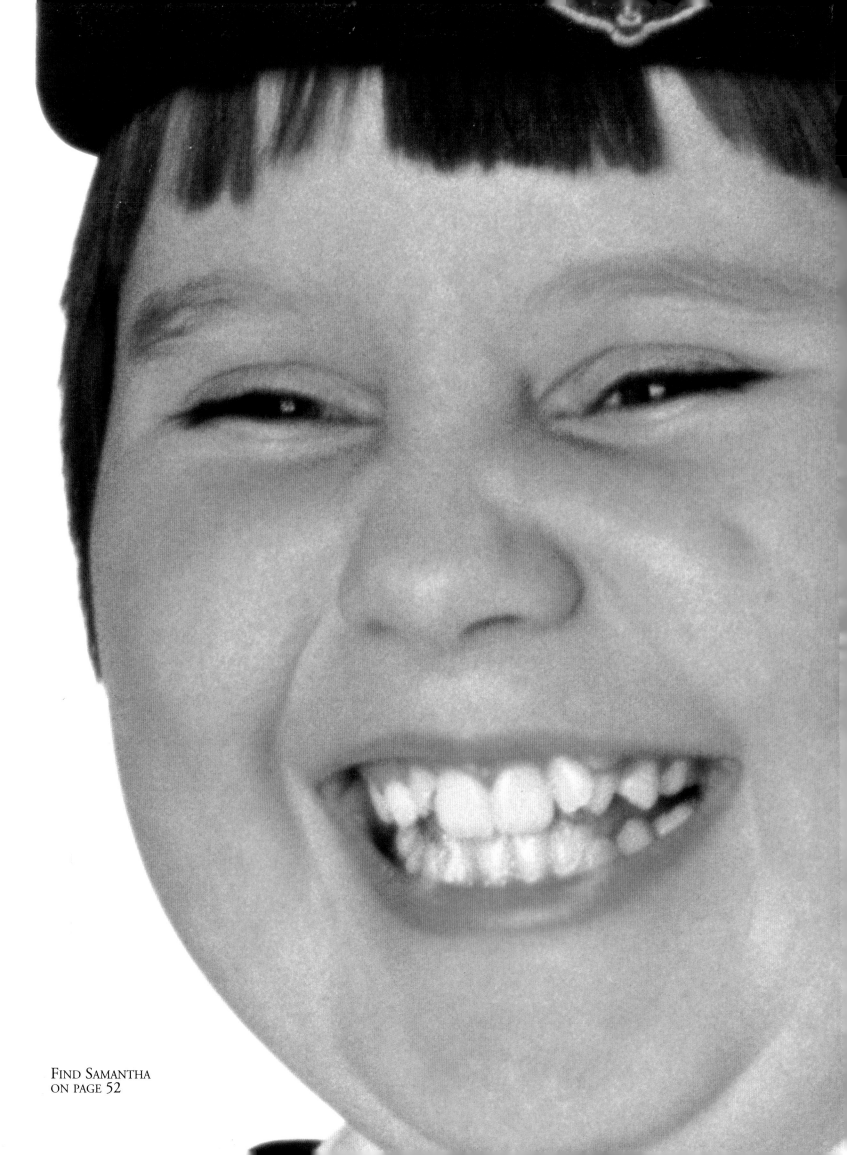

FIND SAMANTHA
ON PAGE 52